Differentiated primary science

Exploring Primary Science and Technology

Series Editor: Brian Woolnough
Department of Educational Studies, University of Oxford

Science is one of the most exciting and challenging subjects within the National Curriculum. This innovative new series is designed to help primary school teachers to cope with the curriculum demands by offering a range of stimulating and accessible texts grounded in the very best of primary practice. Each book is written by an experienced practitioner and seeks to inspire and encourage whilst at the same time acknowledging the realities of classroom life.

Current and forthcoming titles

Differentiated primary science

ANNE QUALTER

OPEN UNIVERSITY PRESS
Buckingham • *Philadelphia*

Open University Press
Celtic Court
22 Ballmoor
Buckingham
MK18 1XW

and
1900 Frost Road, Suite 101
Bristol, PA 19007, USA

First Published 1996

A catalogue record of this book is available from the British Library

ISBN 0 335 19576 8 (hb)   0 335 19575 X (pb)

Library of Congress Cataloging-in-Publication Data
Qualter, Anne, 1955–
    Differentiated primary science / Anne Qualter.
       p.   cm. — (Exploring primary science and technology)
    Includes bibliographical references and index.
    ISBN 0–335–19576–8 (hardcover)   –   ISBN 0–335–19575–X (pbk.)
    1. Science—Study and teaching (Elementary)—Great Britain.
  I. Title.   II. Series.
  LB1585.5.G7Q35   1996
  372.3′044—dc20   95–47949
                                                                   CIP

Typeset by Graphicraft Typesetters Limited, Hong Kong
Printed in Great Britain by St Edmundsbury Press,
Bury St Edmunds, Suffolk

Contents

List of figures and tables

Tables

Series editor's preface

One of the great achievements in the educational system of England and Wales over the last decade has been the growth of science and technology teaching in the primary school. Previously this had been weak and spasmodic, often centring on the nature table and craft work; now it is well established in the curriculum of all children from the age of 5. Primary school teachers are to be congratulated on this achievement, building their science work on often uncertain foundations. This is therefore an appropriate time for this series of books which looks in detail at what has been achieved, and seeks to develop the fundamental principles that underlie the ways in which children learn and teachers teach science and technology in primary schools.

Two approaches to primary school science had been developing prior to the introduction of a National Curriculum. The first saw investigations as the focus of the children's work, studying aspects of their natural environment to develop both an insight into the underlying science and the way that scientists work. The second approach was modelled more on the way in which science had been taught in the secondary school and centred on the content of science which needed to be taught. When the National Curriculum for science was introduced in 1989 it sought, not entirely satisfactorily, to bring together these two approaches, with half the curriculum being given to explorations and investigations and half to the content of science. In this series we are seeking to explore primary science and technology further. We perceive science and technology as more than an accretion of skills and knowledge but rather as a holistic activity involving pupils' hands, minds and hearts. For the pupils to fully learn and appreciate science and technology they will need to develop their attitudes, experiences and knowledge through activities which challenge and stimulate them, and in which they find success and satisfaction. We seek both to educate children *in* science and technology and *through* science and technology, helping them both to appreciate and enjoy these subjects and through them to develop their personality and sense of self worth.

Doing science and technology is a very personal and individualistic matter. Learning science, like the learning of everything else of real worth, is a messy, unpredictable but ultimately satisfying process. One of the benefits of a National Curriculum is that it establishes the place of science and technology in the curriculum. One of the great weaknesses of the English National Curriculum is that it has prescribed the content around an assessment structure which infers linear progression foreign to the way children really learn. Children learn (differentially according to their aptitudes and strengths) by personal exploration; by testing out their ideas in discussion and writing; are being encouraged when they are on the right lines and corrected when they seem to be heading off in the wrong direction and by using the language of science inappropriately. The teacher's vital and sensitive task is to provide the appropriate stimulation in scientific and technological contexts, to allow the children to express their thinking, and to encourage and correct them as appropriate. In such a way children will construct their own understanding and attitudes to science and technology and become members of the broader scientific and technological community.

Anne Qualter's book on differentiated primary science brings together the findings of recent research and her own experience in a perceptive, sympathetic and wholly constructive way. Her refreshing use of real classroom situations carries conviction and gives an authoritative 'ring of truth' to her arguments. Her approach to differentiation in science teaching is both practical and stimulating. She recognizes the 'untidiness' necessitated by the individuality of the different pupils and the expertise of the teacher in fine-tuning lessons as they develop to fit the pupils' growing appreciation of their science. She gives realism and hope to what, in some of the idealistic rhetoric directed at teachers, can seem impossible demands. This will be an important, readable and influential book. It will add much to the development of science teaching in schools.

Acknowledgements

On one of those occasions when half the children in the neighbourhood seemed to have come to tea, my son yelled 'My rice pudding's gone blue.' 'No,' the nine year old opposite replied, 'The light is bouncing off your T-shirt and on to the rice, so it just looks blue.' This just goes to show that what children learn in school they do use outside. I would like to thank all those children who have over the years shared their ideas and views so readily with me. I would also like to thank the very many teachers who have allowed me into their classes and have given a great deal of their time to talk to me. In particular, I am most grateful to the teachers who worked with me recently. They are Sue Andrews, Linda Auld, Iola Edwards, Brian Gilbert and his staff, Joanne Hall, Val Jones, Sarah Robb, Gail Webb and Gwyneth Williams. My thanks are also due to my husband John for all his support, and my children Clare and Liam for interrupting so much. I am grateful to Routledge for granting permission to reproduce models from Gott and Mashiter and Harlen *et al.* and to Open University Press for permission to include an extended quote from Bentley and Watts.

1

The place of differentiation in primary science

Introduction

The primary phase of education in the UK (for ages 5–11 years) has over the past thirty or so years undergone many changes. One of the central tenets of primary education came from an influential report in the 1960s. The Plowden Report (1967) stressed the need to see the child as the centre of the education process. The emphasis on meeting the needs of the individual, of responding to the interests of the child, was central to the way primary education was perceived. This is not to say, of course, that all primary classrooms were models of progressive education. There is plenty of evidence to suggest that much traditional teaching, particularly in English and mathematics, continued (Simon 1981; Galton 1995). However, the primary ethos was clearly that of a caring child-centred approach to the education of young children. Differentiation was not a term regularly used, but within the notion of good primary practice it was axiomatic that children would receive different experiences in school according to their needs. In recent years in England and Wales there has been an increasing emphasis on differentiation in the primary school. Teachers feel that it is problematic and struggle to find ways to ensure the provision of differentiated learning opportunities within their planning. Why is it that differentiation is so difficult to achieve when child-centredness has been the focus for so long?

When the National Curriculum Council (NCC) set up an evaluation of the implementation of science in the National Curriculum in 1991 (Russell *et al.* 1994), one of the requirements was to consider the appropriateness of the science order for more able, less able and talented pupils at secondary level (ages 11–14). Differentiation, it was thought, was not a problem at primary level. Yet since then differentiation has become a crucial issue in both primary and secondary schools. It is one of the main issues considered by the Office for Standards in Education (OFSTED), which is the body responsible for the regular inspection of schools. In a report on science in 1993–4, inspectors were on the whole positive about science in primary schools. They were less than positive about differentiated provision across the whole primary phase; they commented on

the limitations of the frequently undifferentiated planning. Some teachers provide extension tasks for the more able but there is little adaptation of worksheets or other written materials to meet the needs of poor readers. In very few cases are those with particular scientific aptitude given specially challenging tasks.

(OFSTED 1995: 15)

In 1992 the *British Journal of Special Education* devoted an issue to differentiation (see, for example, Weston 1992). In the early days of the National Curriculum it was within the field of special educational needs that the notion of differentiation was being discussed. However, since then differentiation has come to be applied to the provision of appropriate learning experiences for all pupils. The Association for Science Education (ASE), for example, has produced a book on differentiation in primary and secondary science, and its starting point is that 'all learners are different' (Versey *et al.* undated). This does not answer the question as to why differentiation should have come to be seen as a problem which must be addressed in the primary school. To see why, we need to chart the development of primary education and the views of teaching and learning it implies, particularly with respect to the introduction of the National Curriculum. By doing this it is possible to see why differentiation has become an explicit part of what is thought of as good primary practice.

What do we mean by 'good primary practice'?

In recent years I have attended many ASE conferences where teachers, advisors and academics present their ideas for teaching strategies and approaches to teaching different topics. At one such conference I heard how teachers could adapt materials and equipment in order to allow children with physical disabilities to engage in 'hands on' or practical science activities. At the same conference I attended a presentation by a teacher concerned with teaching earth sciences. Both presenters summed up their approach by saying that what they were suggesting was 'nothing more than good primary practice'. Bentley and Watts (1994) sum up their five main tenets of 'classroom constructivism' thus: 'In part, these five points are simply good practice.' These statements were intended to persuade the audience by appealing to a consensus view held by the profession of what constitutes good practice. But what is it? Only by exploring what this means and how science fits or does not fit into notions of good practice can we begin to examine the role of science in the curriculum. The approach taken to teaching any area of the curriculum must depend on the view of what constitutes appropriate curriculum content and appropriate teaching strategies.

In England and Wales the proposal for a distinct phase of education for young children was made by the Hadow Committee, which reported regularly throughout the late 1920s and the 1930s. The aims of primary education in an industrialized society, the report stated, were to go beyond teaching the child to read and write and manipulate numbers, to teaching the child what every wise parent would want for their own, to teach the child how to live his or her life. Hadow did not suggest moving away from imparting knowledge, but did see the purpose of primary education as much broader than that. The reports stressed the wide variety of differences between individuals and indicated that teachers would need to focus more on individual needs than previously (Hadow Report 1931). Some years later the Plowden Report (1967: para. 1229) further emphasized the focus on the individual:

> We found that the Hadow report understated rather than over estimated the differences between children. They are too great for children to be tidily assigned to streams or types of schools . . . Whatever form of organisation is adopted teachers will have to adapt their methods to individuals within a class or school.

The shift in focus from the subject-centred, authoritarian approach to teaching children was not unique to the UK; it was a movement taking root in many countries. In the USA it was seen as the way to bring children up in the culture of a democratic society. 'There need be no fear of "progressive education" when it deals positively and realistically with the assets and liabilities of the individual child' (Gesell and Ilg 1965: 391). The emphasis on the needs of the individual continued to be seen as central to the ethos of the primary school. Norman Kirby (1981: 11) listed the four basic ideas on which the changes in primary education had been founded:

1 Respect for children and their work.
2 The idea that human beings are different from one another.
3 Experience as the basis for learning.
4 The importance of the environment, since environment is the only part of the nature–nurture duality that can be improved by a teacher.

This view has not receded with the introduction of the National Curriculum, but is alive and well in the minds of educators at all levels. Her Majesty's Inspector for Wales, in an extract from his Primary Science Committee lecture at ASE, wrote: 'Education is to do with the individual not with the mass, the essential person not the representative individual' (Evans 1994: 18–19).

Good primary practice might be seen as following a policy of addressing the needs of the individual, a principle that has been part of the rhetoric of primary education for almost as long as primary education has been in existence. So why the fuss now? If teachers have been doing it for years, and teachers generally support the idea, why is it that now that differentiation is the word being used, teachers are concerned to learn how to do it?

The answer might lie in the nature of the changes that have been made to the primary curriculum and the confusion this has caused about the purposes of primary education.

The basis on which a curriculum is built

Blyth (1984) put forward an analysis of the various philosophies which might underpin primary education. He identified three types: the 'process approach', the approach based on 'forms of understanding' and the 'social imperative approach'. The process approach was the one favoured by Blyth. He suggested

> that it regards understanding as constructed anew by every learner, with the accumulated intellectual achievements of mankind as a principal part of the available cognitive resources rather than as an imperative that must be obeyed when curriculum is developed.
>
> (Blyth 1984: 30)

The focus in this view is firmly on the learner. The teacher's role in the process of educating children was to provide them with the environment in which to develop and grow. Subject areas, in this view, are inappropriate because they would limit the freedom of teachers to follow the interests of the children.

The forms of understanding approach is based on the view that there are a number of ways of thinking that are natural to human beings. The different forms of understanding are, however, distinct from one another. These forms include mathematical, linguistic, scientific, moral and aesthetic. The argument goes that they are not distinct subjects, but, because they are important forms of understanding, the subject areas have tended to grow from them. This close relationship between forms of understanding and subject areas was used in the development of a structure for the national performance monitoring programme in England, Wales and Northern Ireland, which began in the 1970s and continued until the early 1980s (Kay 1978). Blyth brushed aside the idea that the forms of understanding would provide the cornerstone for curriculum development at the primary stage, saying that 'it seems more realistic to speak of historical or scientific understanding at the age of 16 than at the age of 6.'

The third approach on which curriculum development might rest is related more to the needs of society than to the development of the individual. This curriculum would base itself on subject areas considered appropriate to the development of a competent workforce. It would promote the sorting of individuals so as to make the most of an individual's potential to meet particular requirements.

It is clear that the basis upon which the primary curriculum is founded must influence both the content of the curriculum and the way in which it is taught. The origins of the development of the primary curriculum in the 1960s, 1970s and 1980s in Britain can be traced back to the Plowden Report. Even a perfunctory look at the report reveals the strong process approach being taken. The arguments against teaching within delineated subject areas were put forward in the report:

> A school is not merely a teaching shop . . . It lays special stress on individual discovery, on first hand experience and on opportunities for creative work. It insists that knowledge does not fall into neatly separate compartments and that work and play are not opposite but complementary. A child brought up in such an atmosphere . . . has some hope of becoming a balanced and mature adult.
>
> (Plowden Report 1967: para. 505)

This is not to say that subject knowledge was not to be part of the curriculum, but that false boundaries were not appropriate where the needs and interests of the individual were paramount. 'The topic may be chosen by the children themselves. The thing to notice about it is that it is likely to cover every "subject" one can think of' (Burgess 1973: 50). Clearly the primary curriculum was being seen as based on a process model. There were, of course, many critics of the approach being taken. These focused particularly on the view that 'the basics' were being neglected in the desire to tend and nurture happy human beings. The evidence did not seem to support such claims. The 1978 HMI primary survey quantified the amount of coverage given to the basics and concluded that primary schools were placing considerable emphasis on reading, writing and mathematics (DES 1978).

In the 1980s Alexander (1984) criticized the prevailing ethos of primary education. Alexander cited the well used phrase, 'I teach children, not subjects.' He argued that we may teach children, but it is important that we teach them something. Eric Bolton, former Chief of HMI, said that 'It is ridiculous to believe that the process could grind away like a coffee grinder without a bean. People do select content. The question is which content?' (*Times Educational Supplement* 3 February 1995). This seems quite obvious, but the fact that the 'something' Alexander had in mind was subjects suggests that he was attacking the basis on which the primary curriculum was built, and offering an alternative, the subject-oriented curriculum.

The idea was developing that primary education ought to throw off the old progressive ideals and become more focused on the teaching of subjects. The introduction of a subject-centred, national, curriculum was part of this. More explicit attacks were made on the approaches taken by teachers and on the child-centred curriculum in general. The Plowden Report was openly criticized by politicians. The woolly minded thinking of the 1960s was waved at primary teachers with exhortations to develop more rigour, and teach by whole-class methods. All this represents an attempt to move away from a child-centred curriculum. In the March 1995 Alan Blyth Lecture at the University of Liverpool, Andrew Pollard discussed the learning environment of children of primary school age. He suggested that the quality of a child's learning depends not only on the delivery of the subject matter, no matter how well it is done, but also on the wider context in which the child learns, his or her home environment and inter-actions with other children, siblings and parents. He commented that the new legislation relating to the National Curriculum has ignored this side of the child and is therefore compromising the possibility for maximizing learning for individuals. Teachers are well aware of this, but are concerned to do their best for the children they teach. In the new climate of testing and assessment this means that children will be judged on their performance on tests.

Within the Early Years department the ethos is such that the development of the 'whole child' is still seen as being implicit in the child's education but a conflict now exists. By Y2 (Year 2 = 7-year-olds) children must have experienced all that is required by all subjects and that we have evidence (or have seen the evidence) to make a Teacher Assessment in all areas. The strain this has placed is fundamental (to the development of the whole child) especially when time is limited and demands are high.

(Key Stage 1 teacher quoted in Rush 1995)

The teaching of subjects needs to be incorporated into concern for the whole child; it should not replace it. Perhaps we should return not to a process approach to the curriculum as preferred by Blyth (1984), but to a forms of understanding view. With this approach, different ways of thinking and learning about the world are provided for within a curriculum which provides for the child as an individual.

The place of science in the primary curriculum

In the elementary schools and primary schools of the 1950s science was not generally considered an important part of the curriculum. This is probably because it had not yet become seen as a valuable asset to the development of the economy. Where science was taught it seems to have been based on nature and the weather. Children learned about plants and the seasons. Teachers encouraged children to learn about nature, to draw it and to keep charts about it. An example from the 1950s describes this.

The work centred around the class nature table and weather chart . . . At first the chart can be a simple set of pictures with a moveable pointer . . . further up the school the chart can take the form of a calender for the month . . . Class nature diaries and nature scrap books of all kinds of things are also made . . . collections are started . . . we have endeavoured to fulfil a need by keeping pets in school . . . seeds such as mustard and cress, grass, peas and beans germinate on blotting paper or in jam jars . . . in winter time just as much pleasure is derived from the lacy patterns the bare trees make against the sky . . . When we find our first snowdrop in the school garden, or the first coltsfoot on the bombed site, out comes our wild flower stand and we begin our flower chart for the year.

(Bush 1956: 12)

Surveys conducted after the Plowden Report had influenced schools indicated that, other than the basics of language and

Table 1.1 Junior schools in the 1970s: curriculum coverage

Curriculum area	Average number of hours per week for pupil	Percentage
Language	7	30.4
Mathematics	5	21.7
Thematic studies	4	17.4
Physical education	3	13.0
Art and craft	2	8.7
Music	1	4.3

Source: Bassey (1978: 28).

mathematics, school subjects as such were not easily identifiable within the primary curriculum. Bassey (1978) was defeated in his attempts to give precise figures for the amount of subject teaching in infant (for ages 5–7) departments (even of the basics), much of the time being spent in 'class talk', 'play time', 'administration' and such like. In junior schools and departments (for ages 7–11) he was able to quantify the different subject areas more clearly (See Table 1.1). In neither the HMI study nor Bassey's study was science found to be considered an important part of the curriculum. Perhaps more importantly, a curriculum consisting of subjects other than the basics was not the basis on which teaching was constructed.

The view of the place of science in the curriculum did shift after Bassey's 1978 report. Although the introduction of science, either as an explicit part of topic work or as a subject in its own right, was patchy, the view of the science which had a place in the primary curriculum was different from that described in the 1950s. Smith (1994) reports on his case study of a primary teacher who, in 1984, said: 'I see my job to give them a wide range of experiences which will enable them to make sense of science with a big S later on' (Smith 1994: 166). Some seven years later, a primary teacher interviewed about science in the National Curriculum said: 'Science has gone from a small s to a big S' (Russell *et al.* 1994). The introduction of the National Curriculum had a major effect. The National Curriculum in England and Wales was introduced in its first form in 1989. It represents a comprehensive prescription of what teachers should teach in each of the ten subjects of the curriculum, and through the use of an eight-level scale of performance outcomes it prescribes what children should know and be able to do as a result of covering the National Curriculum. The shift in the way science is viewed (from a small 's' to a big 'S') within the primary curriculum is crucial. Science was seen as part of the whole experience of the child. Indeed, many teachers would not have identified those aspects of their work which promoted the development of scientific thinking as being science. A topic was rarely analysed into component parts, as this would not make sense when a process approach to the curriculum was taken. It is interesting to think back to the introduction of the National Curriculum and to the ways in which science was then presented to teachers on INSET courses. I heard many an advisor or advisory teacher say that National Curriculum science was only what teachers had always done, but now they were labelling it. The imposition of the requirement to 'label it' signalled a shift away from the process approach to the primary curriculum. Perhaps the advisory teachers felt that, prior to the National Curriculum, science had been developing a different role in the primary curriculum, that it was becoming a recognizable part of teachers' plans, because it was coming to be seen as an important form of understanding to be developed in children of primary age.

Smith (1994) discussed the changes in science teaching which have been brought about by the introduction of a prescribed National Curriculum for England and Wales. The science curriculum lays heavy emphasis on the content of science to be learned, breaking that content down into attainment targets, which, after several revisions, became titled: Life Processes and Living Things, Materials and their Properties, Physical Processes and Experimental and Investigative Science. Smith indicates that a shift had been in the air just prior to the introduction of the National Curriculum. The shift had been bringing the content or knowledge and understanding base of the curriculum under closer scrutiny. The research in science education being undertaken at that time emphasized the concepts of science, but within the framework of a view of learning that was essentially child-centred (Osborne and Freyberg 1985). HMI was encouraging the introduction of science into primary education (DES, 1978), but the pressure was more on the processes of science than on the content for its own sake. In its criticism of the state of primary science the HMI report of 1978 signalled an emphasis on the processes of science.

Few primary schools visited in the course of the survey had effective programmes for the teaching of science. There was a lack of appropriate equipment, insufficient attention was given to ensuring the proper coverage of key scientific notions; the teaching of processes and skills such as observing, the formulating of hypotheses, experimenting and recording was often superficial.

(DES 1978: 33)

It would seem that the shift, in terms of the way science was viewed, was towards a forms of understanding basis for curriculum development. The introduction of the National Curriculum further emphasized the view of science as a way of thinking. Science is one of ten subjects which form part of the English and Welsh National Curriculum. It was given the status of a 'core' subject along with English and mathematics. The science curriculum is described under four areas, which broadly represent the science subjects of biology (Life Processes and Living Things), chemistry (Materials and their Properties) and physics (Physical Processes), with the addition of the processes of science under the heading 'Experimental and Investigative Science'. Four stages of compulsory education were identified as key stages, with Key Stage 1 running from 5 to 7 years and Key Stage 2 from 7 to 11 years. For each key stage a programme of study describes what must be taught from each attainment target for each key stage. Thus, for example, within the life and living processes programme of study for Key Stage 1, pupils should be taught 'to name the main external parts, *eg hand, elbow, knee* of the human body'. The National Curriculum in science has, to date, been revised twice, but still remains quite detailed and specific about what children should be taught and what they should know and understand as a result of that teaching. Thus the eight-level scale of performance outcomes for life processes and living things includes at Level 1 that pupils 'recognise and name external parts of the body using words such as head or arm'. A comprehensive system of assessment is linked to the National Curriculum, with a requirement for teachers to assess their pupils against the outcomes provided and, in the core subjects, against externally set end of key stage national tests.

Although the concepts of science to be covered in the National Curriculum at each key stage were spelled out in detail (set out as attainment targets), at the primary level 50 per cent of the time was to be devoted to the processes of science (described as Attainment Target 1 of the science National Curriculum). It was the inclusion of the processes of science which was used to justify its status as a core subject, along with English and mathematics, in that the skills of science would underpin and allow access to knowledge and understanding in a range of subject areas. 'Scientific method is needed throughout the rest of the curriculum and adult life' (NCC 1989).

The status of science has changed over the course of the implementation of the National Curriculum and its assessment. By further moves towards the adoption of simple paper and pencil tests, the assessment of science processes has been reduced. This has changed the emphasis of the subject, and moved it further away from its role as a core subject 'providing an essential grounding for other learning experiences'. The move towards the testing of content, rather than the processes of science, has resulted in a shift in the status of science, even from the point of view of policy-makers. Although it retains its official place as a core subject, it is not now assessed through standard tests at the end of Key Stage 1 (5–7 year olds), and it does not have equal status with 'the basics of literacy, oracy and numeracy . . . These skills are fundamental to all other learning' (Dearing 1993b). Thus, in policy as well as in practice (because teachers teach to the tests), National Curriculum science has moved into a position where its presence in the core cannot be justified in terms of its general contribution to learning across the curriculum. Justification for its presence in the core can now only be made in terms of its importance to the economic development of the nation. It seems that, despite the best efforts of many of the people who worked on its development, the curriculum is now based on what Blyth referred to as a 'social imperatives' approach. Such an approach does not lend itself to a concern for the development of the individual, but on providing enough people who are sufficiently capable to keep the economy healthy. This is a very depressing view, but not, I am sure, one held by teachers. Most teachers retain a concern for individual development. If this remains so, then it is important that science is seen as a form of understanding to which all children can be given access and from which all children can benefit.

I have argued that the place of science in the curriculum has moved significantly during the past two decades. Like other subject areas, it had no specific place in the primary curriculum of the 1960s and 1970s other than making its contribution to the cognitive resources available to the teacher as he or she supported the child through the process of learning. The shift towards a forms of understanding view was under way, with the emphasis in science being on the processes of science: science as a way of thinking. The National Curriculum began the politically inspired shift towards the curriculum built on the 'social imperative' approach. Such a curriculum does not focus on the needs of the individual. Rather it focuses on the subjects to be taught. The way in which the subjects are to be taught is strongly implied by the often used word 'delivery'. If the view of knowledge is one of packets of information, then the view of the learner is that of a receiver of packets. The packets simply need to be properly wrapped and carefully delivered. Perhaps this is one of the reasons why, when training courses in primary science have been provided, the emphasis has been firmly on topping up knowledge, not on how to teach the subject. One initiative by the Department for Education was to provide funding for in-service science courses of 20 days' duration for primary teachers. This funding was made available to bidders who were offering to teach teachers science, but was not provided for those wanting to teach teachers how to teach science. The concern about teachers' background science knowledge lead to the development of a series of self-study books for teachers, each focusing on one aspect of science (Schilling *et al.* 1991). I was involved in writing the first of these books, the brief for which was to write science for primary teachers, not for children. The view was, it seems, that teachers only need to know the subject to be able to teach it. This view does not coincide with that put forward by many researchers internationally, which is that teachers do need background knowledge, but that they also need to know the subject in a form in which they can teach it (Shullman 1986; McNamara 1991).

The role of the teacher

The teacher in the early part of this century had a very clear role to play: to pass on knowledge, with an additional socialization role. In the period after Plowden the role shifted to that of nurturer, the gentle provider of enriching experiences, along with the basics of English and mathematics. The views of many teachers are still that they need to cater for 'the whole child', but criticisms of this view are constantly being raised. Following the implementation of the National Curriculum, teachers were concerned that it was too broad for them to do any of it justice, and that because it was so huge there was nowhere in the week where they could respond to those children whose needs did not directly coincide with the demands of the curriculum. Sir Ron Dearing (Head of Schools Curriculum and Assessment Authority) sought to redress the balance with his review and subsequent revision of the National Curriculum. The slimming down of the National Curriculum provided, in theory, the equivalent of a whole day per week for teachers to use as they saw fit. This move, which was undertaken after extensive consultation with teachers, was intended to demonstrate support and understanding towards the profession. Unfortunately, no sooner had the new curriculum been introduced than Chris Woodhead, the Chief of Her Majesty's Inspectors of Schools, raised concerns that standards were not higher, suggesting that this was because teachers were still holding on to outmoded practices and perspectives from the 1960s. So where does this leave teachers?

Teachers are still concerned with teaching children. The National Curriculum is concerned with teaching subjects. Thus teachers need to be concerned with teaching subjects to children. The problem is that the two parts of the sentence come from very different views of teaching and learning. Teachers have to find ways to stick with their own beliefs while accommodating the demands of the politicians. The struggle to find a way to do this tends to be embedded in discussions about how to cover the content of the National Curriculum. In science this causes grave problems and hours are spent by teachers planning together, trying to find ways to teach children in a way that meets the needs of the individual while also covering enough of the content. Some schools have felt obliged to move further than is comfortable towards the subject-centred approach.

> Prior to National Curriculum we did a lot of hands on investigative science. A lot of that has gone because the staff feel very restricted by the content, there isn't half the imaginative stimulating stuff going on. The exploration, the practical

has gone. For all sorts of reasons my staff feel, from AT2 [Attainment Target 2] to the end, that they have so much content to get through that the exploration takes second place and we do far less than we used to. It should be more about how they approach science getting them to question. Infant education is about attitudes, independent thinking, not about amassing facts.

(Headteacher)

Many schools retain an emphasis on experiential learning and simply accept the fact that they cannot cover everything. Many schools designed lists of aspects of the curriculum which needed to be covered, checking off with a tick or a dot each point on the list as that aspect was delivered to the children. These tick lists were a source of great irritation for some teachers.

You might spend a long time doing one set of work and you've only coloured in one dot and you've only covered one part of one Attainment Target but the children have got a lot out of it and I think that's important. That's better than doing a bit . . . and the children not really understanding or remembering anything.

(Class teacher)

The role of the teacher at the time of writing, and probably for a long time to come, is developing in schools and classrooms up and down the country, as teachers continue to wrestle with the attempt to assimilate two competing sets of values. Teachers will not simply roll over and play dead, because they invest so much of themselves in their job (Nias 1989). It might be useful for us to go back from the view of teaching as delivering a body of knowledge to seeing the purpose of teaching as teaching children how to use different ways of thinking about the world. There is a way to look at the world from a scientific point of view, and to explore it in a scientific way. It is also important that children are taught to look at their world from an artistic or poetic point of view, to see it as aesthetically interesting and to have the skills and understanding to explore the world in this way. Children need to be taught how to think mathematically and historically. These are important elements in the well educated individual. In terms of science education this means that an overemphasis on content must be avoided. As Harlen (1993: ix) suggests,

> There is always the danger of the pendulum swinging too far, in this case, of the recognition of the importance of conceptual understanding being interpreted as a case for focusing on learning *about* content rather than learning basic ideas *through* content.

What do we mean by differentiation?

There are lots of definitions of differentiation, and the numbers of definitions are increasing dramatically. If we take the 'child-centred' view of primary teaching, differentiation is about addressing the needs of children in ways that are appropriate to the individual (Lewis 1992) and accepting that the needs of the individual may be many and varied. The focus is not simply on the subject learning needs of the child. 'Differentiation is therefore seen as the process of identifying, with each learner, the most effective strategies for achieving agreed targets' (Weston 1992). This kind of view was reflected in the Records of Achievement (RoA) movement, which grew up in schools in the 1980s. Children defined their own personal goals, with the help of the teacher. These might have been to tie a shoelace, to complete a page of sums, to be nicer to the dinner ladies. The child would then decide whether he or she had met that goal, and place some evidence in his or her own record to show this. This reflects a view of education as relating to the whole child as an individual. Where the focus is on subject teaching assessment would be concentrated on the specific knowledge or skill he or she had gained. Many primary schools retain RoAs and still value them as something that the child has ownership of. But some have added a 'pocket', or section, to the RoA, in which the teacher places evidence of work assessed against National Curriculum criteria. This represents an attempt to accommodate the two views of the primary curriculum and its associated assessment. The model for assessment within the National Curriculum has as its focus the subject areas of the curriculum. The whole thrust of assessment is related to finding out the child's position in terms of how much or what in particular the child knows.

The suggestion that differentiation has only two forms – differentiation by task and differentiation by outcome – reflects an assessment-led, subject-centred view of the curriculum. Surely, whenever we set a task to a pupil we monitor how the child reacts to it and, when it seems appropriate, intervene, either to help the child along or to add to the task in order to stretch the child further. Thus differentiation by outcome, where all the class are set the same task, becomes differentiation by task, because the teacher modifies the task for the individual. A teacher decides to intervene for a variety of reasons: the child looks bored, or is messing about; the child looks worried; the child had trouble with this kind of task last time; the child may not have understood. These are not all related to the child's level of achievement, they are related to who the child is, what motivates and interests her or him and the abilities she or he brings to the task. Differentiation is therefore a process that teachers employ while they are teaching. It is part of the process of teaching.

Differentiation that is child-centred and differentiation that focuses on the curriculum are not necessarily incompatible: what matters is where the emphasis is placed. I hope in this book to develop the theme of differentiation in primary science as addressing the learning needs of individuals as they develop their ability to think scientifically.

2

What do we mean by ability in science?

Introduction

Although science in the primary school in the UK has come relatively recently, this does not mean that it does not have a long tradition. This tradition can be traced to curriculum development projects in the 1960s and 1970s, such as Nuffield Science (Nuffield Foundation 1967) and Science 5–13 (Harlen 1975), as well as some earlier initiatives:

> It is our hope that the articles comprising this pamphlet will stimulate discussion and constructive criticism . . . and encourage the spread into Primary school, of work in that creative activity of the human mind which we know as science.
>
> (Science Teacher's Joint Sub-Committee 1959)

Nevertheless, until the introduction of the National Curriculum in England and Wales (DES 1989a) many schools did not give science a place in their curriculum. This meant that there was not

Table 2.1 Teachers' confidence in understanding how children's understanding develops

	Very confident 1	2	3	4	*Not confident at all* 5
English	24[a]	51	21	3	0
Maths	18	54	22	3	0
Science	5	35	46	11	1

[a] Percentage of respondents (n = 508).
Source: Russell *et al.* (1994: Volume 1, 225).

the pool of expert practitioners in schools helping to develop this aspect of the curriculum, as there was in those areas of the curriculum which had been more commonly taught in primary schools. In a study of teachers' implementation of National Curriculum science it was found that teachers were less confident about how children's understanding develops in science than they were in English and maths (see Table 2.1).

In the same survey it was found that 34 per cent of primary teachers felt ill-equipped to teach science. Despite all this, primary teachers do seem to have taken up the challenge. With the help of some in-service courses primary science is steadily developing and taking a place as an important part of the curriculum. In one of its first reports on aspects of the curriculum the Office for Standards in Education expressed satisfaction with the way science was developing in primary schools (OFSTED 1994). The expertise in teaching science is developing.

Grouping in science

Recently I asked a group of teacher training students, who were spending time observing in different primary schools, to find out how teachers group children for science. Not one of the 53 students saw children grouped by ability for science. This matches the findings of larger studies, which note that children tend to work in groups according to reading ability, or English or maths performance. In my own experience of visiting many classes,

Table 2.2   The relationship between performance of pupils in different aspects of the curriculum (Correlation coefficients for 30 children)

	English	Maths	Reading
Science (overall)	0.40	0.28	0.22
PC1 (investigations)	0.60[a]	0.71[a]	0.51[a]
PC2 (content knowledge)	0.44	0.24	0.23

[a] Significant correlations.
Source: Willson and Willson (1994: 15).

seating tends to be by some measure of general ability, or teachers encourage children to sit in friendship groups. With the introduction of the National Curriculum and its associated assessment arrangements, teachers are tending more towards grouping by 'ability'. Yet at the same time teachers often say that a child whose reading ability or mathematical skills are not so good can come into his or her own in science. It is worth asking the question of whether it is appropriate to use maths or language performance as a measure of general ability, or of ability in science. Sally and Mike Willson looked at children's scores on maths and English standard tests, and on NFER reading tests. They compared these scores with pupils' performance on the knowledge and understanding of science (Attainment Targets 2, 3 and 4 of the science curriculum) and found no correlation between any of the scores and performance on the knowledge and understanding of science tests. Interestingly, however, performance on the first attainment target (investigations) did correlate with scores on the English, maths and reading tests (see Table 2.2).

There are many reasons why teachers place children in fixed groups for much of the time within the classroom. Many use some form of integrated day. One group might be working on language tasks while another is doing a science investigation, and another is working through maths books. This allows teachers to make the best use of scarce resources. The most valuable of these is the teacher's time. If one group is working on an activity that needs little teacher attention, the teacher is released to work with another group whose demands are higher. Children also get used to working with the others in their group and are more relaxed and happy as a result. Yet the temptation is to see the members of any one group as homogeneous in terms of their ability in all areas. I doubt if any teacher would agree that this is the case with any group in a class. The problem remains that teachers need to be able to provide each child with opportunities to learn that are appropriate to that child.

As part of a research project to evaluate the implementation of science in the National Curriculum, a large sample of teachers from across England was interviewed about teaching science (Russell *et al.* 1994). Many of these teachers raised their concerns about judging ability in science. Teachers often cited the child who in most situations is considered less able, but who shows real ability in science:

> I have a boy in my less able group, his reading and writing are not good at all; but in science he really shines. He has lots of ideas and can think of ways to test them. The trouble is he falls down on recording, so I can't give him the higher levels, because I know he won't do so well in the tests.

The individual children mentioned so often in discussion highlight a dilemma for teachers that goes beyond concern about individuals. The fact that these children seem to be bringing something to science lessons that is not required by other subjects raises a number of questions about what is valued in the science curriculum, and what skills, knowledge and understanding are appropriately brought to science learning by children. The question then is: what makes science special or important in the education of children? What does it contribute in particular to their general education?

Teachers' views of primary science

While discussing differentiation in primary science, an experienced teacher expressed her concern that young children should not be stifled by the need to make detailed written records of their science work. Science, she believes, is 'about doing'. The processes of science are the crucial element of the subject. These sentiments echoed many of those made by primary teachers when they were asked about the nature of science in the primary phase:

> I think of its value as a part of the curriculum . . . I have got children who, like George . . . he hates writing, he hates

English, he hates maths and will rush through everything, but he loves ... science. I like science because it gives them the opportunity to find out things for themselves ... They do something and then they tell me why it happened. It's the same, like technology really, not to learn facts, although that's part of it, but it's learning the processes, it's learning the processes of learning.

(Teacher of 8 year olds quoted in Qualter 1994b)

Teachers see science as a 'hands on' subject, where children learn by doing. The focus of much primary science prior to the introduction of the National Curriculum in England and Wales was on the processes of science, rather than the content. Although as early as 1978 Wynne Harlen was asking the question 'Does content matter in primary science?' (Harlen 1978), the focus of almost all the science done in primary schools was on the processes or skills. Where science was successfully introduced into local education authorities (LEAs) and into schools it was because teachers were warming to a kind of science that was not like the science they were taught in school. This science fitted in with the primary ethos of experiential learning, and at the same time did not challenge teachers' knowledge and understanding of a subject that many had dropped at a very early age. One teacher, when asked about the value of her own science background, was almost surprised by the question:

Do you mean the science I did in school? You mean what I did; it isn't relevant to what I am teaching ... I don't remember doing any of the sorts of things I do with these children. I think I would have remembered but I never. Science was boring, we didn't do practical, so there was nothing practical, which would have appealed to me more.

Many teachers of primary science value the subject as a part of the curriculum because they value the processes of science rather than specific scientific concepts such as 'forces' or 'the Earth in space'. Teachers' focus when teaching science tends to be on areas that lend themselves to practical work (McGuigan *et al.* 1994). The introduction of science as a core subject within the National Curriculum was predicated on the value of science being in the processes involved.

The three core subjects encompass essential concepts, knowledge and skills without which other learning cannot take place effectively. Competence in language, numeracy and the scientific method is needed throughout the rest of the curriculum and adult life.

(DES 1989b)

The notion that science should be 'hands on' is one almost universally expressed by primary teachers. It fits in with their general view of how children learn, with the idea that it is the processes of science that are important. However, it is important to consider the phrase 'hands on' more carefully. Is it that children need to be working only with things, with their sleeves rolled up floating and sinking objects, or rolling cars down slopes, or planting seeds and measuring them as they grow? How do we ensure that they are developing the concepts of floating and sinking, of forces or of growth? I have no doubt that children learn best by doing, but also by talking about their ideas, and by exploring those ideas in a variety of ways. To use another cliché, children's science work needs to be both hands on and minds on. An example of some work undertaken in a Key Stage 1 classroom illustrates this point.

A year 2 (6 year olds) teacher found that children in her class did not know where seeds came from and how they generate new plants. She began by discussing the seeds and the children's ideas about where they come from. She decided to make the link straight away with other life cycles that the children had already worked on, in particular the chrysalis and the butterfly. The teacher started by bringing some flowers, including some that had gone to seed into the classroom.

Teacher: We have brought this into the classroom too. What is it?
Cara: Chrysalis.
Teacher: What will it become?
James: A butterfly.
Teacher: Now we want to see how a seed goes round like the caterpillar. How it goes all the way round? (Describes a circle in the air). Now look at your seeds.

The teacher used observation of plants with the children, who then made drawings and cut up flowers to look inside. They were encouraged to talk about their observations, developing appropriate language. They could then use this extended vocabulary to discuss the similarities and differences between the flowers they were studying. The children noticed that all the flowers they had looked at had similar structures inside them. They found out that these were related to the seed boxes. The class watched a television programme about flowers and seed production. The children did some modelling of flowers using plasticine. It became clear, looking at their models, that the discussions about flowers, seed boxes etc. had focused the children's observations, enabling them to model detailed flower structures:

> that sort of stimulated things, they started using the right sort of vocabulary as they went along, whereas previously they were struggling to find the right sort of vocabulary to express themselves, and the drawings are becoming more detailed.

Once the children had developed their understanding of the structures in flowers and how these are related to seed production they were able to find appropriate information in books, because they had developed a clearer understanding of what they were looking for. They began to point out the flowers on trees and to discuss the idea that apple trees flower before producing apples.

The above example demonstrates the link between exploration involving actual objects, the development of concepts and the associated language to describe these concepts. One way in which this was done was to encourage the children to make their observations concrete by modelling them in plasticine. Simply cutting up flowers without the teacher pointing out the structures involved, and without her helping the children to see the similarities between different flowers, would not have led the children into making the connections and would not have developed their understanding of the concepts. 'Hands on' as a way to describe good primary science is not enough; it is the interaction between the hand and mind that is important. This is a model that tends to be used in the area of technology rather than in science (Kimbell *et al.* 1991).

Although teachers tend to value the 'hands on' approach to primary science, there is a recognition that children will not learn processes in isolation from content. Content is important, as is the interlinking of process and content. This is perhaps the challenge now facing those teachers who have developed their confidence and competence in teaching science. How can children be provided with the opportunity to progress in their understanding of both the procedures and the concepts of science? If this question is to be answered there is a need to begin not just to look at the curriculum as it is written down, but also to consider how children's understanding develops, and how teachers translate the curriculum to support individuals' development. This book explores some issues with respect to the support for individuals in developing their understanding. Discussion is based on a view of the teaching and learning of science that needs to be made clear at the outset.

How children learn science

As described above, many teachers have warmed to teaching science because they believe that it fits in with the way children learn. The science they are talking about is the 'hands on' science of the primary school and not really the science they learned in school. Many teachers, when discussing the nature of learning in science, referred back to Piaget and his stages of development. Piaget's view was that thought is internalized action, and that the analysis of human knowledge and intelligence must begin with a consideration of motor activity and practical problem solving (Wood 1988: 19). This resonates well with teachers' commonly held view that science should be hands on.

Teachers identified their children as being at the stage described by Piaget as concrete operational thought; they are, therefore, unable to think in abstract terms and need direct experiences in order to learn. 'A child reaches a level when it can reason, until it can reason you can't do things that involve reasoning, things have to be done at a simple practical level' (primary teacher quoted in Russell *et al.* 1994). It was for this reason that many teachers found teaching about the Earth and space counter to their views of good practice. They could not see any practical way to teach about the solar system that did not require children to make abstractions, which they felt would be beyond them. Piaget's theories were a very important part of my training to be a teacher twenty years ago, as they were for many others before and since. However, although his theories are not discarded, much has been learned about learning since and these theories have been developed much further, perhaps beyond all recognition. Certainly the notion of fixed stages of development between which thinking is qualitatively different is open to question. Teachers of experience are aware that children may be capable of very sophisticated thought in one area of the curriculum and not in others. This is because children bring their interests and experiences to their work. Their own learning has progressed in some areas more than others. It is clear that children do not fit neatly into Piagetian stages in their learning, and that more sophisticated explanations are needed.

One of the most persuasive criticisms of Piaget's theories came from Margaret Donaldson (1978). Much work had been done, using Piaget's theories, on children's responses to problems, including work by Donaldson and her colleagues. Her book *Children's Minds* represents a reinterpretation of the findings of Piaget and others. She suggests that children are much more capable of thinking and are much less restricted by the Piagetian stages of development than had hitherto been suggested by Piagetian researchers. Her argument was that, because children have an understanding of human contexts, they are capable of very sophisticated reasoning when operating in real, human situations.

One of the experiments used by Piaget and others to indicate whether a child has reached the stage of 'operational thought' involved showing a child a set of objects, such as flowers, where six flowers were red and two were white. The child is then asked 'Are there more red flowers than flowers?' Children under six tend to say that there are more red flowers, although they often qualify this with 'because there are only two white ones'. Piaget argued that this type of response indicated that the child could not deal with the idea that the red flowers are a subset of the flowers. However, I suspect that those readers who read this question for the first time initially thought the answer was: more red flowers. In part this is because we have an expectation of the kind of question that is being asked and our attention is drawn to the two kinds of flowers. Donaldson gives some examples of tasks that are fundamentally the same as the flower task, but where the researcher placed the emphasis in the question on the set and not on colours. In these cases a significantly greater proportion of young children could answer the question correctly. It seems, then, that a child's response is determined by the way the question is asked and how far he or she relates it to a real human question.

The context in which a question is posed and in which a task is set influences the kind of response made by an individual. Often in science teaching it is suggested that a relevant context, something within a child's experience or grasp, results in greater learning because the task motivates the child. Donaldson's work suggests that it is something rather deeper than that. When a task is placed within a human context that is recognizable to children, they are put in a position where they can access what they know, and can make links with other situations and contexts. In such cases children's thinking is likely to be far more soph-isticated than, for example, Piaget might have predicted.

The constructivist view of learning

Much recent research into children's learning in science has involved the constructivist view of learning. This view describes learning as an active process involving the selection and integration of information by the learner (Wittrock 1974). It is very much the opposite of the view that people are empty vessels to be filled with knowledge. People are said to construct, to build up, their own concepts, a concept being an idea or set of inter-linked ideas that a person uses to explain his or her experi-ences and observations. We also use our ideas about the way the world works to make predictions about what will happen. To use a trite example, if we notice that each day the sun goes down, and in the morning it comes up again, we can use this to predict that tomorrow the sun will come up. A person could have a concept of the Earth as a place on which we live; she may, because she has seen pictures, think of the Earth as round. Many children and adults hold this view, but have difficulty integrating this with their own experiences of living on a seemingly flat Earth. Many children think of the Earth as round and flat, like a button (Nussbaum 1985). By thinking of the Earth in this way, the children are able to integrate the information they have been told, and see no reason to question, with their own experiences. These ideas are not dissimilar to those found on old maps of the world, where people assumed that the Earth was flat. They had no idea what might be beyond the edge, so they added the warning, 'Here be dragons.' There comes a point when ideas cannot be tested simply against accumulated experiences, but must be tested empirically (going to look for the edge of the world!).

The ideas that people develop often arise from their everyday experiences and observations. Explanations that heavy objects fall more quickly than lighter objects are derived from and reinforced by everyday experiences (Watts 1983). Children develop an everyday understanding of a word, which they then apply inappropriately in the context of science. Children's descriptions of what is under the ground revealed that some believe that there is an apple core at the centre of the Earth (Russell *et al.* 1993). The persistence of these ideas are an outcome of experience with the world (Caramazza *et al.* 1981). A great deal of research has been undertaken on children's ideas in science. It has been found that certain ideas appear often; children are making sense of the world in similar ways. Children must therefore be having similar experiences to deal with and try to explain, even in different parts of the world. However, it is common for English children to draw sound travelling in similar ways to the way it is depicted in comics (Watt and Russell 1990). It is unlikely that children in parts of the world where comics are not available will use such forms of representation. In another example, the Primary SPACE project reported that when children in England were asked to explain why they decided that certain objects were alive, or not, most primary aged children mentioned movement and growth, and, to a lesser extent, feeding or nutrition (Osborne *et al.* 1992). When similar questions were asked of school children of the Buddhist hill people in Nepal, the most common response was in terms of whether or not something breathes (Hanson and Qualter 1995). Most children in both samples were quite accurate in classifying living and non-living, but the reasons for doing so were different. The differences between the children may well be to do with their religious and cultural backgrounds.

The constructivist view of learning is that new concepts are the result of a building on to existing ideas as a result of new experiences (Posner *et al.* 1982). The implication of the model for teachers is that, by responding to and challenging the initial ideas of children, they can help them to construct a new understanding that is more scientifically useful; that is, an understanding that has greater explanatory power. Sometimes new learning cannot be reconciled with earlier learning, and accommodation, in which

Figure 2.1 Child's drawing of Earth in space

existing concepts are reorganized, must take place. Learning therefore depends upon existing knowledge, since it is this that helps the learner to decide what sense to make of new experiences. The following is an extract from a lesson on the Earth in space with a mixed class of year 3 and 4 children (7 and 8 year olds). As part of a research project looking at progression in understanding, the children had, some time previously, been asked to make drawings of their ideas about the Earth, planets and how day and night occur (Russell *et al.* 1994: Volume 2). Two of the children's original drawings are reproduced as Figures 2.1 and 2.2.

The teacher decided that he needed to work with the whole class to look at models of the movements of the solar system, using the overhead projector as a light source. However, the lesson was designed to relate back to children's initial ideas, and to encourage them to challenge their own ideas. The teacher reminded them that day has followed night ever since they were born, even since he was born, and even long before Jesus was born.

Figure 2.2 Child's drawing of Earth in space

Teacher: Now, what were your first ideas about why that is?

Helen: Because summer nights are longer than winter nights.

Teacher: Well Ben, can we use your idea? (Nod from Ben.) Ben's idea was that the sun is a ball in the sky. Remember, Ben? Another idea was about clouds. Tell me Lisa, what was your idea?

Lisa: I thought the clouds go over the sun to make it dark.

Teacher: What did we do?

Lisa: Looked outside and it was cloudy, but not dark.

The topic is one that many teachers find difficult to reconcile with their views about how children learn and about what primary science is. Yet the teacher managed to encourage the children to think about their own ideas and challenge them. In some cases the children's ideas could not be so easily checked, but the teacher showed the children photographs from space telling them that people had been there and suggesting that the children might like to reconsider their ideas in the light of this evidence. In this kind of learning environment children are encouraged to use secondary sources and to consider ideas other than their own, to compare these ideas with their own and consequently to develop their own concepts. The approach taken by this teacher accords well with the findings of Gunstone *et al.* (1992), who claim that encouraging pupils to think about what they think promotes conceptual change.

The development of procedural knowledge

The above example of teaching and learning is based on a constructivist view of learning, but it does not come within what many teachers would mean by 'hands on' or investigative science. The investigative process in science, that which justifies science being considered part of the 'core' of the National Curriculum, can be seen as the route through which children learn scientific concepts such as energy or respiration, and as a set of concepts in their own right; for example, the awareness of the need to control variables in order to ensure that the question being asked is likely to be answered, or the awareness of the need to link data arising from an investigation to the original question being addressed. Concepts of the procedures of science (procedural knowledge) need to be developed in the same way as concepts of the knowledge of science if children are to have the procedural tools available with which to develop their ideas. In the example of the children learning about night and day, the class were exploring their ideas and fitting their own experiences to these ideas. They were able to raise questions and to check them out, by looking at a cloudy sky. The procedural knowledge was being developed by the teacher along with the content knowledge.

Prior to the introduction of the National Curriculum in science much of the emphasis was on the development of process skills. The DES policy statement of 1985 underlined this: 'pupils need to grow accustomed from an early age to the scientific processes of observing, measuring, describing, investigating, predicting, experimenting and explaining' (DES 1985: para. 24). The statement went on to encourage a problem solving approach to science learning. Much emphasis was placed on the skills and processes of science, individually and combined, for the purposes of problem solving. Often assessment of science was approached through the assessment of the individual process skills. The Assessment of Performance Unit (APU) identified six categories of science performance that could be measured. These were using graphical and symbolic representations, use of apparatus and measuring instruments, observation, interpretation and application, planning of investigations and performance of investigations (Russell *et al.* 1988). In a survey in 1984, the APU found that the skill rated as most important by teachers in England, Wales and Northern Ireland was the ability to observe carefully, followed closely by 'the enjoyment of science-based activity' and 'a questioning attitude'.

The work of the APU demonstrated that the assessment of the various processes of science in isolation was not necessarily a good predictor of how a child would perform when undertaking a whole investigation. The other five categories of science activity assess processes that may be involved in carrying out an investigation, but the sum of these parts does not necessarily make the whole (Russell *et al.* 1988: 85). The lessons from the APU project were that children are likely to develop an understanding of the procedures of science and how to apply them through doing whole investigations, rather than learning separate skills on the basis that they will then be able to assemble them when attempting to solve a problem. Practical work other than whole investigations has a place in the National Curriculum for science. Practical work is used to illustrate an idea so that the child can understand the science concept better. So, for example, a teacher might want to reinforce the idea that a complete circuit is needed for a bulb to light. He or she would give children a set of circuit diagrams and ask them to state which is complete and which not, to construct them and find out and so demonstrate that a complete circuit is needed. Practical work can also be used to help to develop particular skills, such as the use of a measuring instrument (NCC 1991). Yet it was the importance of learning both procedural and content knowledge through doing whole investigations that the first version of Attainment Target 1, Exploration of Science, attempted to promote.

The first version of the National Curriculum (DES 1989a) was heavily influenced by the view that the ability to solve problems and perform investigations was 'more than the sum of the parts'. Thus, the attainment target for investigative science subsumed the skills of science under the heading of 'Explorations'. Within this was mention of skills and processes, observation, recording, planning, measurement, drawing conclusions, using secondary sources etc. These were all seen as part of the ability to develop an understanding of how to explore scientifically. This was seen as different from learning skills in the same way that one might learn to use a screwdriver. Instead, it was seen as knowledge of the procedures of science. In the same way that one can develop knowledge and understanding of sound and how it travels, it was argued that people develop knowledge and understanding of the procedures of science. That is, the processes of science have a conceptual base, just as other aspects of science have. Qualter *et al.* (1990) proposed a model to describe the interrelationship between children's developing procedural knowledge and their developing conceptual knowledge. They depicted procedural and conceptual development proceeding on parallel paths, with links being made through investigations or other explorations by children. This seems to make the assumption that procedural and conceptual knowledge develop together at the same rate. So if this model is interpreted too literally, then, as Carré and Ovens (1994) point out, the level statements in the National Curriculum for science, for a knowledge and understanding attainment target and for the investigations attainment target should map on to one another. This would be expecting too much. Rather, it may be that a pupil's level of development in one may limit his or her progression in the other. If a child does not have an understanding of sound travelling, he or she will not be able to develop a successful investigation to find out which is the best string telephone. On the other hand, a child who has no understanding of a fair test could not develop an understanding of how sound travels by investigating string telephones. However, this is not the same as saying that children's understanding develops in parallel.

Another model, which has been developed more recently and upon which the 1995 version of the science National Curriculum (Department for Education (DFE) 1995) seems to be based, refers to aspects of science such as those described by Feasey (1994):

1 Skills, including using equipment, measurement, constructing tables, making graphs.
2 Processes, including observing, hypothesizing, interpreting, inferring, drawing conclusions.
3 Knowledge and understanding, under which three attainment

targets of the science order are listed: Life and Living Processes, Materials and their Properties, and Physical Processes.

Arching over these is procedural knowledge. This maps on to the 1995 order for science, where 'Systematic Enquiry' that involves children being given the opportunity to 'ask questions (e.g. 'How?', 'Why?', 'What will happen if . . . ?') has been separated from the attainment target on Experimental and Investigative Science. In the attainment target pupils should be taught 'planning and experimental work' (which includes recognizing a fair test), 'obtaining evidence' (including using measuring instruments) and 'communicating evidence' (which includes making graphs, tables and charts). The separation of processes and skills is not complete, but the element that represents the whole investigation is now moved out of the attainment target structure, implying that investigative science does not need to be assessed through whole investigations, although such assessments are still officially expected.

None of the models of investigative or procedural science mentioned above attempts to explain the relationship between processes and concepts in terms of the way children learn. If the constructivist view of learning is adopted, and we accept the notion of procedural knowledge, then it follows that the development of an understanding of how to investigate should be explainable in terms of constructivist theory. Gott and Mashiter (1994) propose a model to explain the development of procedural and conceptual understanding (Figure 2.3).

This model suggests that, as a child is presented with a problem, or raises one, he or she tries out certain things in an attempt to make sense of the problem. In doing so children rely on their understanding of both the processes and concepts that are inherent in the problem. When they address these problems their understanding of the concept develops, as does their understanding of the processes involved. The example given below may serve to illustrate this model in action, and to highlight the role of the teacher in supporting the development of both procedural and conceptual understanding.

The following excerpt is from a lesson in which one group of year 6 (10 year old) children were attempting to find out which material would be the best insulator; this was linked to their topic on explorers. The pupils had already set up the basic

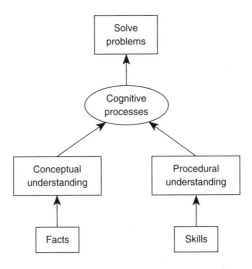

Figure 2.3 A model for science. From Gott and Mashiter (1994)

experiment, which was to find which material was the best thermal insulator. They had found paint tubs and had designed lids for them through which thermometers could be fitted. They were then thinking about planning their experiment and how they would gather the data. The teacher checked with them that they had developed a reasonable plan before allowing them to fetch hot water and begin their experiment. One child started by asking where the measuring jugs were kept because they needed the same amount of water in each.

Teacher: Why do you think it is important to have the same amount of water?

Philip: To be fair.

Teacher: Yes, but why in this experiment?

Philip: Heat escapes quicker for lesser water.

. . .

James: Sir, water takes longer to boil when there is more of it, so if you had different amounts of water then the one with less in it might cool down quicker than the one with more – the heat would go out quicker.

Again the teacher accepted the answer, and said that this is what the other pupil had meant, but commented on the fact that the argument was well thought out.

The teacher in this class was concerned that the children saw the reasons for the fair test. He did not simply accept the answer 'to be fair', but probed them about why 'fairness' is important in this experiment and what that 'fairness' should involve. The link between process and concepts is clear here, as the teacher endeavours to develop the children's concept of 'the fair test' the children needed to bring their understanding of heat and energy to bear on the problem. They needed to think carefully about what they meant by a fair test. The two were intertwined. In supporting the development of the concept of a fair test the teacher had also supported the development of the children's understanding of heat and insulation.

Black and Harlen (1993) discuss the interplay between process and concepts in terms of two main aspects, categorization and transformation. In the case described above, the two children could categorize the problem they were presented with as about heat and heat loss. The second child could transform his knowledge to make predictions: 'it takes longer to boil a larger amount of water than a smaller amount, therefore it would take a larger amount of water longer to cool down than a smaller amount.' Black and Harlen suggest that the ability to identify the appropriate concepts to use in solving problems is one of the main stumbling blocks to children moving forward in their understanding. The context of a question restricts their view of the possible concepts to draw on to solve the problem. It may be something like trying to find a particular book in a very large library. If I am given the title of a book to look for, such as *Rites of Passage*, I don't know whether to look in the section on religions, anthropology or fiction. If I am told the name of the author, William Golding, I might, if I know something about the author, be fairly sure that I should look in the fiction section. If I have never heard of the author, having his name won't help. I may have lots of knowledge about different things, but selecting which knowledge to access to solve a particular problem is easier with clues from the context. However, if the context gives the wrong clues it can send you along the wrong track. One example of this effect is quoted in APU reports. Thirteen year olds were set a problem. They were asked to imagine themselves stranded on a mountain in cold dry conditions. They were then asked to find out which of a selection of materials would keep them warmest. The idea was to set a context for an experiment similar to the one the children quoted above were doing. However, in their responses to this question many children began to describe building a shelter, setting a fire going, sending up flares for rescue parties. The context had cued these children into lots of ideas, the least important to them being which was the warmest material. I will discuss the effects of context further in Chapter 4.

The development of procedural knowledge is not well understood. There has been much more research directed at how children's knowledge and understanding of scientific concepts develops. Yet this is an area of science that many teachers, particularly primary teachers, value and wish to develop. In talking to primary teachers and in watching lessons I have come to the conclusion that practitioners probably know a lot more about how children's procedural knowledge develops than do the educational researchers. It is just very hard to disentangle.

Learning as a social activity

O'Loughlin (1992) argues that the suggestion that pupils actively construct their own interpretation of events neglects the social context in which learning takes place. Children do not learn all by themselves but as part of a society. It follows, of course, that if children bring their ideas to school, they must have learned them somewhere, and often it is from listening to others, from conversations with others, both adults and children. The ideas children develop as members of society are not only those related to science, or to other school subjects. They also develop ideas about how to behave, ideas about what it is valuable to learn and what it is not, and ideas about what is relevant to them and what is not. Essentially people learn within a social context. Margaret Donaldson (1978: 88) puts it even more strongly: 'Indeed personal relations appear to form the matrix within which his [the child's] learning takes place.' The following example deals only with one tiny piece of science learning – quoting richer examples of social interactions would take up more space than is available here.

A group of Year 5 children (9 year olds) had been looking closely at different sugars in order to develop an hypothesis about which sugar would dissolve most. The teacher was not with the group, but the thinking went on.

Jonothan: Is it what you think will be first and why? (This
               was a general question directed at the group.)

Haley: No. It's really about how you are going to find
               which is the best at dissolving.

Jonothan: We could look at five minutes and decide the one
               which has dissolved the most.

Michael: We could time how long? We could take a table-
               spoon of each.

Jonothan: We need to make it fair. We could crunch up the
               sugar cube to make it fair.

Haley: Then it won't be a sugar cube, it will just be nor-
               mal sugar.

Here the children were exploring their ideas together and so
were able to formulate their experiment together. The children
were clearly aware of the need to make a fair test, and needed to
explore that. They were able to do this within the group because
they had developed appropriate social skills to use to exchange
ideas and learn from each other. Jonathon was, according to the
teacher, the least able member of the group. He might not have
come to an understanding of how to make the test fair if he had
not had the support of his peers.

Promoting progression in science

There exists a vast body of research on children's ideas, and
there has also been some work done on strategies for promoting
conceptual change. Posner *et al.* (1982) suggested that there must
be dissatisfaction in the child with existing ideas, and new ideas
should be intelligible and plausible. The excerpt from the lesson on how day and night occurs exemplifies this: the teacher
actively encouraged the children to make their ideas explicit and
to compare them with further evidence and other ideas. Once
children begin to feel that their ideas might need thinking about,
they need to be provided with opportunities to explore the incon-
sistencies of their models and subsequently seek new models that
have more explanatory power. What is the role of the teacher
in promoting progression in children's understanding? When
the first non-statutory guidelines for science were being written,
a common conception of the role of the teacher was that of

facilitator. The teacher provided an environment and experiences with which the pupil could interact, and so develop. This view of the teacher rarely found favour with any of the teachers I talked to at the time, and some found it quite insulting. Yet if the ideas of Piaget and the view of learning as resulting from an interaction with the environment are appropriate then the teacher can only be seen as a facilitator. If, however, the constructivist model is extended to include the notion of learning taking place as a social activity, then the teacher, as much as any other person, can be part of that society from whom the child draws ideas. The teacher then adopts the role of facilitator and resource. It is possible to see the role of the teacher as much more central to the learning of the child if Vygotsky's theories of learning are considered.

Vygotsky, like Piaget, believed that thought and action are closely related. One important difference between the two was that Vygotsky, like Jerome Bruner, set much more store in the influence of social interaction on learning, while Piaget focused mainly on the interaction between the child and its physical environment. Vygotsky believed that children have certain things they can do or understand entirely alone, and then certain things that, with help, they will be able to do. The support of others to achieve success that would otherwise be just out of the child's reach is where much learning takes place.

In the following example a mixed-age class of 5 to 7 year olds (25 children in the class) were studying materials and change as part of a topic on houses and homes. They had a small collection of bricks and stones in the class and were going to take a trip around a small local brickworks to observe the process. The teacher believed that, for the children to make sense of their observations as they went round the factory, they needed to come to some understanding of the process beforehand. Prior to the trip the teacher worked with groups of about ten children discussing their ideas, starting with looking at a house brick.

Teacher: What do you think this brick is made of?
Sally: It's out of clay.
Simon: Where do you think the clay comes from?
Esme: You just dig it out of the ground.
Teacher: Where would you find some clay?
Sally: It's in the school.

John: Under the soil.

Teacher: Yes it's very clay soil here, so you would see it here.

Marc: They just get it out of the ground, then they shape it to bricks and they cook it.

Teacher: What do they cook it in?

Josie: An oven.

Teacher: Can you think of anything else that is changed by heating?

[Lots of responses: a cake; cups are made hard in an oven; food like meat, plastic things; some things have to be in really hot ovens.]

Josie: A hot oven like they have got in the juniors.

Teacher: Does anyone know what they call the oven?

Manahz: A kiln.

Teacher: Do you think they use a kiln like the one in the juniors at the brick works?

Manahz: No, it would be this wide. [Most of the children stretch their arms out wide saying, 'it would be two metre sticks, no three, ten . . . twenty-five . . .']

Teacher: So, we know that they bake clay in a kiln. But I went to the brickworks last week and I found that they don't get their clay out of the ground, they make it.

Sally: How do they do that, miss?

The teacher showed the children some small pieces of shale and encouraged them to inspect it. The stones were then wrapped in a piece of cloth and hit with a hammer. The children then inspected the dust.

Teacher: But how would I make this into clay? [The children were baffled.] How do you make cement?

Marc: You add water and then mix it. I helped my Dad to . . . and you put it in a big bowl and it stirs it around.

Esme: That won't make clay if you add water to it.

The teacher invited the child to add a few drops of water to the dust, and the resulting clay was passed around for inspection. 'So that's how they do it at the brickworks.' The teacher went on to explain that they dig up shale, grind it and add water.

The class went on to discuss the reasons why the clay needed to be fired: 'It would ruin the wall paper if it stayed wet,' 'If you fell on the wall you would leave shapes in it.' They also considered how the clay might be shaped. Initially they thought it could be shaped by hand, but then suggested other ways: using a mould, shaping it with rulers like patting butter. As a child made a suggestion they tried out the idea using some dough.

One child said, 'I've got a shape maker at home for play dough.' The child explained what a shape maker does (it is a toy that extrudes different shapes of dough). Then the children looked around the classroom for something with a shape they could extrude the dough through. They found unifix cubes and proceeded to make 'square sausages'.

The teacher drew the discussion to an end by encouraging the children to think about the stages they might see in the process of making bricks. On the following day they arrived at the brick-works, and a group of children were overheard discussing their immediate observations.

Alison: Why have they got chimneys?
David: For all the smoke to get out.
John: No, the heat has to get out, you wouldn't have smoke.
Alison: You might have smoke if you burnt the bricks.
John: But you just cook the bricks, you don't burn them do you?
David: Perhaps they don't use the chimneys any more, they might use gas ovens not wood fires nowadays.
Selina: Miss, I can hear a scraping loud noise!
Teacher: Sounds like something being tipped.
Anna: I bet it's all the stones being poured off that dumper truck (see Figure 2.4).

The teacher here found that the children in the class understood that clay is baked to produce brick. They needed little support in understanding this. However, they did not understand that clay is related in any way to rock. Thus the teacher was able to support them in developing their understanding. She encouraged the children to make suggestions and to try out ideas. Individuals were able to make connections with their own experiences outside school and were able to share these with other children, who, although they may not have made concrete with

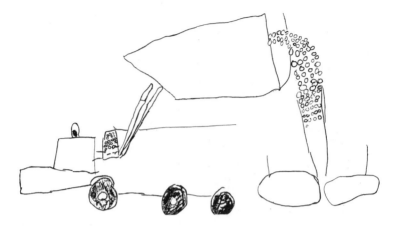

Figure 2.4   Dumper truck dumping stones

their fathers, had some experiences of this process so that they could grasp the idea. The teacher in this case used discussion initially to find out what the children did know, then used this as a starting point to scaffold their understanding, through making links with other experiences, so that in the end their knowledge was extended. They demonstrated the following day that they had grasped these new ideas and were able to use them to make sense of the situations they observed (see Figure 2.5).

In another (Year 5) class the children had been planning and trying out an experiment on dissolving things. The teacher had, over the previous few weeks, focused her attention on developing children's recording skills. She had on this occasion decided to leave the children to try to develop their own. She observed the groups as they struggled with this, before deciding that some children were not going to get there on their own. She said, 'This is the point where I have to go in and teach them.' In this case the teacher was using 'teach' in a very particular way. She meant, it seems, that certain children had reached the point where they could not move forward without her support. Next time the children might be able to achieve success alone. Recently researchers have again become interested in this notion of supported development or scaffolding.

The idea of a point in the child's learning where movement forward can be achieved with the support of a teacher is a useful one for exploring the role of the teacher in promoting progres-

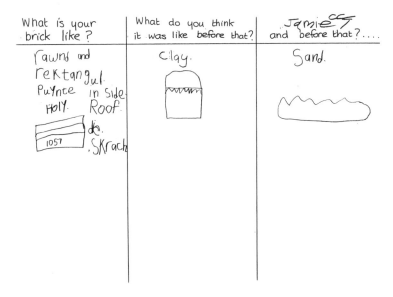

What is your brick like?	What do you think it was like before that?	Jamie and before that?....
rawnd and rektangul. Puynce in Side Holy. Roof. 1057 SKrach	Clay.	Sand.

Figure 2.5 The origins of a brick

sion in children's understanding. The teacher is not, in this view, seen as the facilitator, or as a resource and facilitator. The teacher is:

1 An analyser of the child's position in his or her learning.
2 The facilitator of appropriately designed experiences.
3 The provider of carefully graduated resources (that includes questioning the child, discussing ideas etc).
4 A supporter of progress.

The teacher therefore needs to diagnose the child's level of understanding in relation to the curriculum. He or she must have a clear understanding of the path that the child should be directed along, and an extensive grasp of the range of possible strategies that could be taken in order to provide the best learning environment. The heavy demands on teachers of this approach to teaching were reflected by a teacher who had just read an article on grouping for differentiation in *Primary Science Review* (Crossley 1991).

> She [the author] is so analytical, she had to know the children and analyse where they were heading, she had to know

the curriculum. I don't know how ordinary teachers could be that analytical; I don't know if I could and I have a science background and have been teaching years!

It must be part of the experience of every teacher to have spent some time in discussion with an individual child, 'seeing how far you can take them'. The child moves forward in his or her understanding slowly, becoming more tentative as the teacher pushes him or her further, until a point is reached where the teacher is fairly sure that the child cannot move forward any further. Some children can get further than others, but there generally comes a point where the amount of effort on both sides is not being rewarded.

So what is ability in primary science?

Although the theories of learning discussed above do indicate that some children may have a greater capacity to learn, it would seem that capacity is influenced by what they already know. What they already know is determined to a large extent by the richness of experiences that they have been afforded at home and at school. Ability, then, is determined by where the child is and what the child's capacity for learning is. The implications of this perspective are that for teachers to support progression in children's understanding successfully they need to be able to assess where the children are and to reassess the children's understanding as learning takes place. Assessment needs to be diagnostic and then formative if progression is to be maximized. The determination of starting points is all important in this.

3

Finding starting points

Introduction

There are many reasons why the same activity results in different outcomes with different children. Some of these reasons are related to the interest an individual child has in the topic. Some are related to the extent to which the child sees that activity as relevant to him or her. One factor that is related to all of these issues is what the child knows and understands already. In this chapter I will explore further the idea that it is possible to start from where children are. I will do this through a discussion about finding starting points, and by thinking about what might be the consequences of finding children's ideas. However, as there are so many other factors that impinge on how teachers conduct their lessons and what children learn from them, I will leave discussion of the teaching that follows finding out ideas to Chapter 5, where case studies provide the basis for discussion of the complexities of carrying on from where they are.

It is all very well people saying 'start from where they are'.

This phrase has become a common cry in science education. The problem is that it can often seem that of the thirty children in a class, only two have similar ideas or starting points. One reaction to this state of affairs might be to develop separate study schemes for each individual. This would reduce the opportunity for pupils to learn from one another and to learn to work with one another, two factors that are most important parts of the science curriculum. The Primary SPACE research project (Russell *et al.* 1993) explored the ideas held by children between the ages of 5 and 11. The reports produced by this project give ample evidence to suggest that, although children's ideas might all look different, it is possible to categorize them into a limited number of groups. This begins to suggest that it is possible to take account of starting points. The skill in doing this is to analyse the responses of children to questions at a very simple level. Before you start to analyse the ideas held by children it is worth considering where these ideas might have come from. The kinds of ideas children hold have been found to be similar, even in different parts of the world. Most teachers develop an ability to predict what some of their children's ideas will be, and will have an understanding of the common ideas held by children. However, it is always wise to be prepared for the unexpected.

Sources of learning

People learn from experience. We take information from many sources and use it to try to explain our experiences. Children might have fewer experiences, and have a narrower platform of ideas on which to build, but like everyone else they learn from experiences. It is not always possible to predict what children will make of an event, partly because they are building on a different 'raft' of ideas from those of the adult. It is difficult to separate out the different sources of experience that influence the development of children's ideas. For the sake of clarity I will refer to three different sources of learning.

Observation or direct experience

The most obvious way for a child to learn is by interaction, or observation of his or her immediate environment. Children will notice that it gets light every morning and goes dark at night. They will use this observation to predict that tonight it will go dark. They will also try to explain what is happening on the basis of their own experiences of the world. So children may come to the tentative conclusion that the sun goes down so that they can go to sleep. Or that the sun goes to bed, like people do. They may come across information in their picture books that owls are awake at night. They may then have to change their ideas to accommodate this new experience. The sun goes down so that people can go to bed and the owls can get up.

Most children in the West have never experienced complete darkness; they lie in their bedrooms at night in 'the dark' and can see objects in the room. It is hardly surprising that they come to believe that light objects can be seen in the dark. Nicholas Selly (1994) reports on a study in which he presented 10 year old pupils with a series of questions about cats in the dark. Most children in the class thought they would not be able to see a dark-coloured cat in the dark, but they thought they would be able to see its eyes. Opinions were mixed about whether a white cat could be seen in the dark. Some children went home and took their cats into dark cupboards to find that they could not see white cats in the dark. They accepted then that even light colours cannot be seen in the dark. The odd thing was that they could not see cats' eyes. This observation was less easily explained by the children: perhaps the cat's eyes were too weak, it being only young? Cats' eyes do seem to glow, and it is quite difficult to believe that the cats' eyes in the middle of the road do not have light bulbs in them. Direct experience is one of the most powerful ways in which we learn and on which we base our interpretations of the world. Once established, children's ideas are not so easy to change (Caramazza *et al.* 1981). In this case the children needed to learn a little more about light and reflection before they could explain why cats' eyes could not be seen in the dark.

Language

There are many examples of how children interpret language literally. If we think about our everyday descriptions of vision we tend to reinforce the idea that seeing is something actively done by the eyes. We look 'daggers', we 'throw a glance'. This use of language reinforces the experiences of children, they have to move their head and their eyes in order to see. In other situations we talk about keeping the cold out. We talk about animals when we mean animals other than humans, so it should come as no surprise that many children do not consider humans to be animals. Children often only equate animals with mammals other than humans. Insects or fish are not referred to as animals. This distinction was explored by Trowbridge and Mintses (1985), who found that children tend to be unsure about the classification of animals that are not typical of the group.

Media

Children also learn a great deal from the media. Cartoons often reinforce and exaggerate the ideas people have. The hero with X-ray vision sends out a ray from his eyes (very active vision). Young children will often be found attempting to beat their shadow in a turn. Peter Pan takes this idea further, and allows the shadow its independence. Very loud sounds can make our ears throb, but in cartoons the idea is exaggerated so that the ear enlarges and throbs visibly in time with the drums. Advertisements often influence children's ideas. Children are concerned about the environment, but it seems that the media can lead them to believe that 'environmentally friendly' products are positively good for the environment. A 9 year old girl described the advantages of such products:

> 'cos if you stop all that [using petrol and moving to lead free petrol] maybe you will do a bit of good to the ozone layer ... and ... er ... all the aerosols you just get one from the Body Shop ... and do more to help the environment.
>
> (Qualter *et al.* 1995)

A teacher recently asked her pupils to draw where they thought the various organs of the body were positioned. One child drew the heart on the arm. This turned out to relate to a campaign by a charitable organization that encouraged people to 'wear their heart on their sleeve', pinning a golden heart on the sleeve to show they had given money.

Sources of learning: synthesis

Of course, children generally learn from all three sources and many others. They ask questions, they have things pointed out to them, they watch television, often programmes that are difficult for them, they go on days out with their parents. They are learning all the time by interpreting their experiences and trying to make sense of them. In trying to interpret their experiences, children often discuss their ideas with others. I have learned a lot about this myself from listening to my children (aged 5 and 7 years at the time) talking to one another. One day we were driving past an oil refinery;

Liam: All that stuff coming out [of the chimneys] is killing the otters in the sea.

Clare: Yes, it's steam and it's making the Earth too warm for them.

Children try to make connections between things to try to make a coherent explanation of a phenomenon. Samuel, a 10 year old child, knew that power stations generate electricity, and knew that the electricity had to have a way to reach his home. He had also heard about other means of generating electricity. His information was incomplete, but he tried to close the gaps. Prior to undertaking a topic on alternative energy, the children in the class had been asked to think about where electricity comes from (Qualter 1994a). They were asked to draw a picture from the light socket to the source of electricity (see Figure 3.1). Samuel's explanation weaves his knowledge about power stations, and his observations of the 'smoke' coming from them, with his knowledge about windmills. He had seen a wind farm when out for a drive with his father.

Teacher: Can I just ask you to explain what's on your picture?

Samuel: This is the power station, and they are all the cables going to the light bulb.

Teacher: What's going on, do you think, in the power station?

Samuel: There is things twirling round with power.

Teacher: Something is twirling round with power, yes, and how? Where does the twirl come from, what makes it twirl?

Samuel: Electricity.

Teacher: Electricity?

Samuel: [Pause.] And wind.

Figure 3.1   Where electricity comes from: Samuel's picture

Teacher: Wind, so you think the wind might make the twirl-
        ers. And you have got these big cooling towers.
        What's this here? You have got this big chimney, is
        it a chimney? [Nods.] And what's this coming out?
Samuel: All the foggy, smoggy stuff.
Teacher: Where does all the foggy smoggy stuff come from?
Samuel: Somewhere in there [pointing to a cooling tower].
Teacher: Do you know what causes it to be made in there?
Samuel: No.
Teacher: Can you think of any other ways that we could get
        to make some electricity to go down these cables?
        Is it just power stations?
Samuel: You can have windmills.
Teacher: And how do they work?
Samuel: The wind goes and they spin round like that.
Teacher: So they have got propellers and they sort of spin
        round.
Samuel: And they catch all the air and make electricity out
        of it.
Teacher: OK. So, if we put a windmill in a sort of container,
        would it use up the air?
Samuel: Yes.

Teacher: And how does the electricity that it makes get from
the windmill to the houses?

Samuel: Miss, I don't know.

Another child in the same class also began by talking about power stations, but quickly went on to talk about his ideas about rocks. It transpired that he had been taught a trick where lifting heavy weights in a particular way would result in the muscles in his arm contracting involuntarily, seemingly pulling the two rocks held in the hands towards one another. He thought there must be some power in the rocks that could be harnessed.

> You could use the like, strongness out of them, and you have got hard rocks, get the goodness out of it. I know a trick like, that rocks got energy, it's the harder the rock. If you take a rock and put it round your arms it's like a magnet when you put two of them together. So, I think that's got a lot of energy in that.

Children develop their ideas from a wide range of experiences, from direct experience, by interpreting language, from the media and from school. The outcomes in terms of what pupils learn are not always those anticipated by the teacher, sometimes because the child has misinterpreted the language, the experience or the information provided by other sources, such as the television or books. A 10 year old child, during a topic on the Earth's place in the universe, was asked to draw a picture to show how she thought the phases of the moon occurred. The class had already studied how day and night occur and how the Earth moves around the sun. She had demonstrated an understanding of these concepts. However, her annotated drawing left the teacher puzzled as she showed the phases of the moon correctly but also drew the full moon with a slice in black separating off. When the teacher asked her to explain her picture, she said that a piece of the moon breaks off and moves in front of the sun, which makes it dark. It transpired that this was her interpretation of a video the class had seen, where an eclipse had been demonstrated. The child had seen a black disc, said to be the moon, move in front of the sun and block it out. The black disc was the bit that had 'come off' the moon when it waned. She had not reverted to a less sophisticated idea about how the phases of the moon happen, but was trying to understand why the disc of the moon was black as it passed before the sun.

Common ideas

As soon as you start looking at children's ideas you are over-whelmed by the diversity of them. Yet as teachers, if we are to find a way to 'start where they are' and at the same time need to fit all this into a sensible classroom management structure, it is essential that we group children's ideas in some way. Interest in children's ideas in relation to the way they interpret their world goes back a long way. In the 1920s Piaget (1929) explored children's ideas about what is 'alive'. He presented children with a range of things, asked them if each was alive and asked them to explain their answers. Based on the evidence from this experiment, he developed a very simple approach to grouping ideas, a hierarchical model of how children's understanding of 'alive' develops.

Stage 0   No concept, random judgements or inconsistent or irrelevant justifications.

Stage 1   Activity. Things that are active in any way (including movement) are alive.

Stage 2   Movement. Only things that move are alive.

Stage 3   Autonomous movement. Things that move by themselves are alive.

Stage 4   Adult concept. Only animals (or animals and plants) are alive.

(from Carey 1987: 17)

Much research using Piaget's methods found that children's ideas fit well into this model. But Carey and others looked a little more closely and used a wider range of activities to find that it was the increased biological knowledge that helped children to develop their ideas about what was alive. As children develop an understanding of the various processes of life (that is, movement, growth, respiration, reproduction etc.) they are able to apply these to the problem of what is or is not alive. Lucas *et al.* (1979) gave children a picture of something found on a beach and asked them to suggest ways in which they might demonstrate whether it was alive or not. Children tended to mention the external features of the thing, such as 'Has it got a mouth?' or 'Does it move?' They also tended to mention more than one life process. This approach provides much more evidence of children's biological knowledge and supports Carey's view that it is the extent

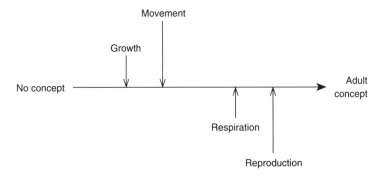

Figure 3.2 A model to show the development of children's understanding of the processes of life

of the child's biological knowledge that influences their decisions about what is alive. It also emphasizes that when one is finding out children's ideas the question that is posed to them determines the nature and quality of the information gained. The evidence suggests that children's ideas on this subject might be grouped in a rather different way, progression from no concept to the 'adult' concept being mediated by the development of biological knowledge (Figure 3.2 shows a model of development in this concept).

Movement is something children can observe for themselves; so is growth, particularly when their own growth rate is being pointed out to children regularly. But breathing might not come into the frame if it is not something they learn about somewhere. The Nepali children referred to in the previous chapter (Hanson and Qualter 1995) must have learned about respiration from somewhere, and so were able to use it in their responses. Teachers wishing to find out about children's ideas about 'alive' would wish to frame their question in such a way as to elicit information about which processes of life the children understood. This would help them to formulate plans for further work exposing the children to ideas about respiration, or reproduction, or nutrition. Teachers might decide to provide children with experiences of how plants move, or look at insects to show how they take in the air they need for respiration, or look at reproduction in flowering plants.

Pam Wadsworth (1994) has developed a way of classifying children's ideas. She suggests the following.

1 Anthropomorphic views: attributing human characteristics to phenomena; for example, in response to the question as to why night occurs, 'the sun goes to bed at night.'
2 Egocentric views: concerned with the child; for example, in response to why night occurs, 'we've got to go to bed.'
3 Colloquialisms: ideas based on what people say or ideas from the media, so the reason why a child can't see at night is that 'he ain't been eating carrots.'
4 Ideas based on limited experience: for example, children represent blood as spots or the body as a hollow cavity filled with blood. This makes sense when you think about what happens when they cut themselves.
5 Stylized representations: some children's ideas reflect the way things are represented in cartoons and story books. For example, light is drawn in straight lines radiating from the sun or a torch. This does not necessarily mean that they understand that light travels in straight lines. On the other hand, many children recently have drawn the sun wearing dark sunglasses after a popular margarine advertisement. This does not mean that they understand the sun to wear glasses, rather that they see this as a convention or symbolic representation of the sun. This is important in a consideration of children's drawings and I will discuss it further later in this chapter.

Pam Wadsworth's grouping of children's ideas can be generalized to a wide variety of concepts. Unfortunately, as far as teachers are concerned, it is more a way of describing the different ideas children have than a way of grouping ideas that will help planning. What would a teacher do differently with a child who says that night occurs so we can go to sleep and a child who says that the sun needs to go to bed? For the teacher the problem is more complex than it is for the researcher. The teacher needs to interpret and group children's ideas in relation to what it is he or she wants the children to learn. So, for example, teachers would not only want to know whether children knew which things were alive and which not, but also what processes of life they understood in order to make their classifications. This would then inform the teacher about what to cover and how to do it. So one might find that most of the children in a class understood movement and growth to be processes of life and could correctly apply them to a range of plants and animals. They might not understand that living things respire, or that reproduction is common to living things. This would inform the teacher about where to go next.

Recent research in the area of children's ideas has focused more on the issue of helping children to change their ideas. The SPACE project was set up not only to discover children's ideas, but, by working with teachers, to attempt to find ways to help children towards more useful ideas. In the case of children's understanding of vision, Osborne *et al.* (1993) present four categories of ideas. These categories are also hierarchical, in that they range from no concept to ideas that approach the scientifically accepted view.

1 Children who provided no explanation about vision. When asked to describe in a drawing how they see a book, the children simply draw themselves and the book.
2 Children who provide explanations without links: They explain, for example, that when the light is on they can see the book.
3 Children who provide an explanation in the form of simple links. This is one of the most common responses of children between the ages of 7 and 11. The child draws or describes a single line between the eye and the object. Sometimes he or she indicates a direction, often from the eye to the object. This implies that the children have a view of vision as active, of eyes as looking.
4 Children who provide an explanation in terms of dual links. Only a small number of children in the age range recognize that there is a relationship between the light source, the object and the eye, thus identifying that light is necessary for vision.

These categories represent a hierarchy, but they are also categories a teacher might be able to use in planning teaching. Those children who had no idea about what is necessary for vision might need to be shown the effects of darkness on their ability to see. Those children who had an idea that light is necessary for them to see the book might hold the view that light is simply there, that there is a sea of light. They would benefit from some exploration of light sources, which things make their own light and which do not. The third group might look at how light needs to be directed so that we might see an object. Thus in a dark room they might find out that the torch needs to be directed to the object that needs to be seen, rather than on to the face of the person who is doing the looking (which is almost invariably their first approach). The last group might explore reflection, considering how light bounces off all objects so that they can be seen. They might also consider different coloured light and why things are seen as having different colours. An eagle-eyed teacher will no doubt notice that, if only one group is going to do something as exciting as going into a very dark cupboard, the other groups would not take it too kindly. So the suggestions touched upon here all involve the dark cupboard, but the activities are different.

If teachers want to be in a position to 'start from where individuals are', there is need to develop strategies for finding out where they are. However, these strategies have to involve some very careful consideration of what it is we want to teach the children, why the ideas are being elicited and what we might then do with these ideas. One strategy suggested above is that, once children's ideas have been elicited, the children can be grouped according to these ideas. This is the most obvious way to differentiate, to provide experiences appropriate to the needs of the individual without giving individual schemes of work. However, it is not the only way. Teachers use many different ways, and for a wider variety of reasons than simply the children's starting ideas. Whatever the intended teaching strategy, finding out children's ideas can be a valuable starting point. In the following section I will consider the different expressions of ideas by children, and consider ways in which these ideas can be grouped.

Analysing children's representations of their ideas

When children are first asked to represent their ideas about, for example, how they see an object, they find it very difficult. In part this is an unusual question, and in part, possibly, they have not really thought very hard about how they see an object. They just can. As they get used to being asked to represent their ideas in different ways, particularly when they feel secure that they are not being tested, they often enjoy the challenge. There are many examples of approaches to finding out children's ideas. However, many teachers find it difficult to use these ideas to help with planning. In the following sub-sections I offer a number of examples of the collection of information about children's ideas and the ways in which this can be used in planning and teaching.

Ideas about living things (analysing children's written work)

A class of 10 year olds had done some work in previous years about living things as part of topics titled 'ourselves' and 'health and hygiene' and in the study of a wild area in the school garden. The teacher's intention here was to move on to develop the children's understanding of the processes of life in relation to plants and animals. The children were to study reproduction in both animals and plants, and would look at photosynthesis. The research discussed above indicates that children tend initially to list movement and growth, and only later include respiration, reproduction, excretion, sensitivity etc. The teacher was interested in the extent to which the class applied their biological knowledge to a new situation. The class was shown a photograph of something washed up on a beach, in the same way that Lucas *et al.* (1979) had done. The children were asked to think of ways they could use to find out if the thing was alive. The strategy adopted here was to ask the children to try the problem on their own, and then to discuss their findings with other children in their group before making a second attempt at a response. In this way children who knew about a particular process, but had not thought to include it on the first attempt, could do so on their second. It is clear that children do learn from one another, and do 'bounce ideas' off one another. In this way the activity was seen by the class as a learning activity rather than as a test. It also provided more information for the teacher. We all know the feeling of thinking of an answer to a question after the event. The teacher wants to know what the children know, not what they can remember about what they know immediately after having been asked the question. Helen's first response is shown in Figure 3.3.

All but four of the class of 27 mentioned movement on their first individual attempt, while only six mentioned nutrition. Fifteen children mentioned nutrition after discussing the problem with others in their group. Helen's second response is shown in Figure 3.4.

Only one child suggested growth: 'See if it grows in a day.' This is not surprising, as the children did not interpret the task as requiring a long time. The teacher was, however, fairly sure

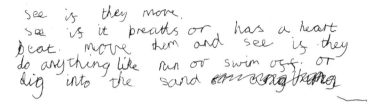

see is they move.
see is it breaths or has a heart
beat. move them and see is they
do anything like run or swim off. or
dig into the sand ~~something~~

Figure 3.3　What's washed up on the beach? Helen's first ideas

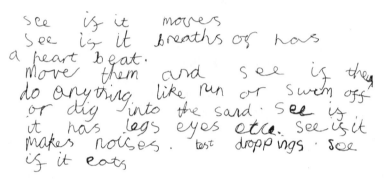

See is it moves
See is it breaths or has
a heart beat.
Move them and see is they
do anything like run or swim off
or dig into the sand. See is
it has legs eyes etc. See is it
makes noises. test droppings. See
is it eats

Figure 3.4　What's washed up on the beach? Helen's further thoughts

that all the class knew that living things grow. As with the Lucas *et al.* research, children mentioned external features such as eyes and mouths. The presence of these features was taken by the teacher to indicate that the thing on the beach could sense light and take in food. Some children could not get away from external features, and were not using these to indicate the processes of life (see Figure 3.5).

There was a wide variety of responses to the question. Only one child mentioned the possibility of the thing being a plant. This again is not surprising, as the children would have little experience of plants being washed up on a beach. A number of children thought the creatures were shellfish of some description, and so suggested X-rays, prising the shell open or tempting the shellfish out with some fish food.

For the purposes of planning, three levels of response were identified:

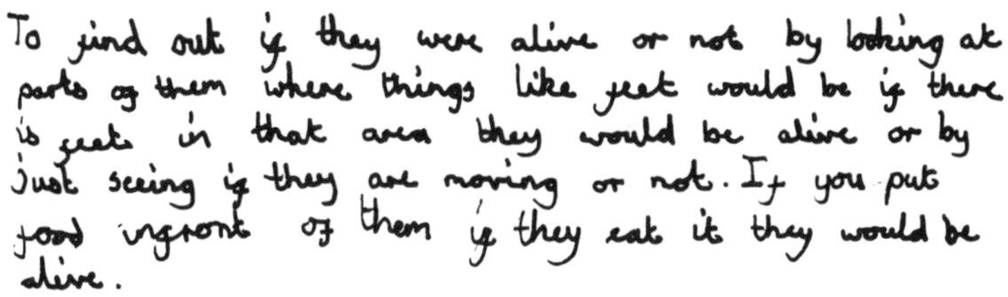

To find out if they were alive or not by looking at parts of them where things like feet would be if there is feet in that area they would be alive or by just seeing if they are moving or not. If you put food in front of them if they eat it they would be alive.

Figure 3.5 What's washed up on the beach? Ben's ideas

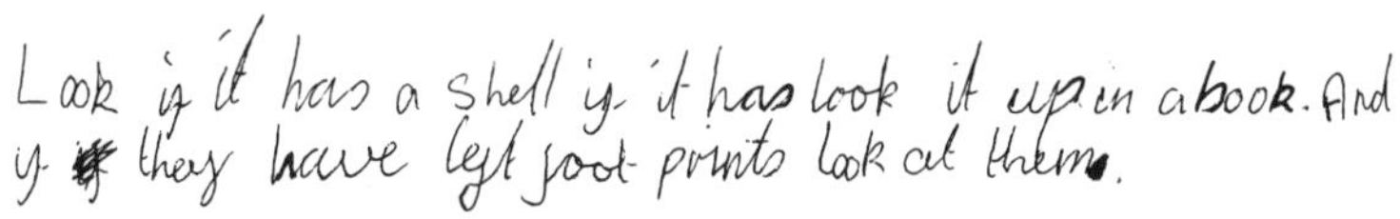

Look if it has a shell if it has look it up in a book. And if they have left foot prints look at them.

Figure 3.6 What's washed up on the beach? Michael's further thoughts

1 No clear idea of the processes of life, no coherent suggestions as to how to find out.
2 Some indication that movement as well as some other processes of life need to be looked for, e.g. sensitivity, nutrition.
3 An understanding that the thing on the beach needs to meet certain criteria based on the processes of life, movement, nutrition, sensitivity, excretion (not all life processes mentioned).

One group of pupils was identified who were unable, even after discussion, to identify processes of life other than movement (see Figure 3.6). Five children fell into this category. The lack of biological knowledge apparent in these children worried the class teacher, who felt that some remedial teaching was essential for this group. She felt that it was unlikely that they would benefit from work on exploring the similarities and differences in plants and animals with respect to life processes. She decided that they needed further experience of sorting living things and studying their characteristics.

A second group of six children was identified who struggled to make a coherent response to the question, although they alluded to sensitivity ('prod it and see if it reacts') and generally to external parts such as legs etc. (see Figure 3.7). The teacher decided that this group would benefit from additional support

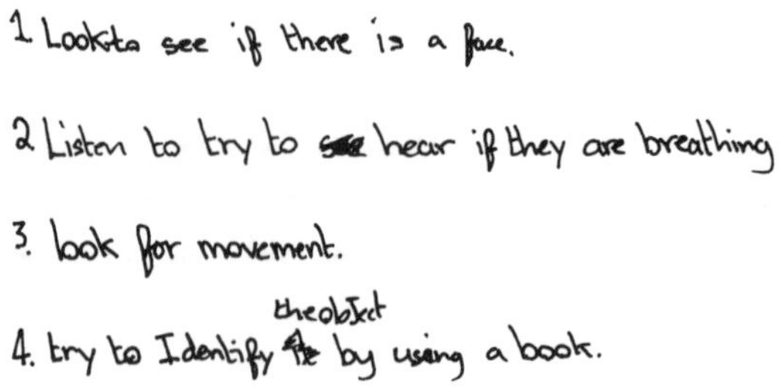

1. Looks to see if there is a face.

2 Listen to try to see hear if they are breathing

3. look for movement.

the object
4. try to Identify the by using a book.

Figure 3.7 What's washed up on the beach? Graham's ideas

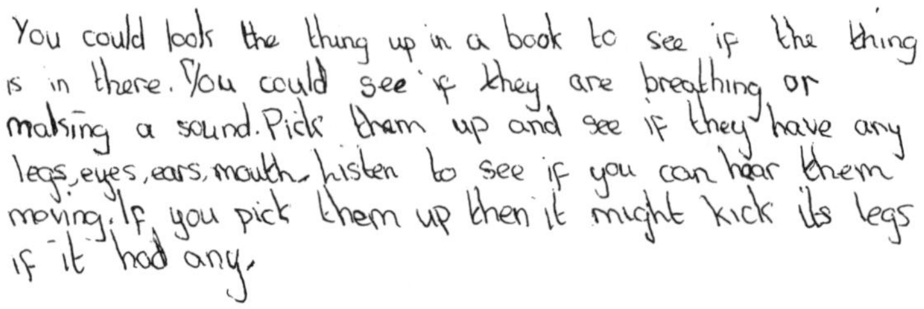

You could look the thing up in a book to see if the thing
is in there. You could see if they are breathing or
making a sound. Pick them up and see if they have any
legs, eyes, ears, mouth. Listen to see if you can hear them
moving. If you pick them up then it might kick its legs
if it had any.

Figure 3.8 What's washed up on the beach? Freya's further
thoughts

in developing their biological understanding. They needed to
look again at the processes of life and to consider what different
organisms need to survive, before moving on to consider the characteristics of plants and animals in terms of the life processes.

The final, and largest, group (17 children) mentioned at least
three life processes in such a way as to convince the teacher that
they understood them. They also included the suggestion that
they would go to secondary sources (books and experts on the
subject) to find out more about the thing on the beach. The class
teacher felt that these children were at a stage where they could
be provided with a list of the life processes as a starting point for
discussion. They would then be in a position to look at animals
and plants and find out how they reproduce, excrete, gain nutrition etc. Much of this work would be possible using books and
other secondary sources, with some input to the group by the
teacher. Helen's responses (Figures 3.3 and 3.4) are very detailed;
Freya also gives an indication that she understands the issues
(Figure 3.8).

Although there was a wide variety of responses, even from the group of children falling into the third category, the three broad groups could be identified because the purpose for which the grouping was being undertaken was clear.

Ideas about sound (analysing children's drawings)

It is now quite common for teachers to be advised to ask their pupils to make a drawing of their ideas about, for example, how we see things, what causes something to move or what happens to the water in a puddle. The problem is finding ways in which the ideas children represent in their drawings can help to determine starting points. Teachers often seem to use the collected drawings to give some idea of the general way of thinking that the children in the class have.

A class of 7 and 8 year olds who had studied sound in their previous class were about to revisit the topic briefly. The class was given a fairly typical drawing task to undertake. They were shown a toy shaker. They were asked to think about how they hear the sound, and then to draw their ideas. As predicted by the research (Russell *et al.* 1994), there were many different ways to represent sound, such as squiggly lines and musical notes. Some used more sophisticated representations, showing sound as waves. Although there was a wide variety of responses, in this class they fell into three main groups;

1 No representation of sound travelling, no notion of sound as having a source. One child responded in this way (see Figure 3.9).
2 Sound represented as having a source, but not as travelling so that the hearer can hear it. Ten children responded in this way (see Figure 3.10).
3 Sound represented as having a source and travelling to the hearer. Eleven children fell into this group (see Figure 3.11).

Some of the last group might have been interpreted as falling into a fourth category, where sound was represented as travelling from a source, in all directions, and being detected by anyone within the area. However, the limited drawing skills of the children and their interpretation of the problem might have prevented some children from making such a full representation of their ideas. A first step for the teacher might have been to talk

Figure 3.9   Representing sound: no indication of sound travelling

to some of these children about their ideas, and to get them to elaborate on them. Teachers often leave the class alone to make their drawings. However, discussion with the children, and encouragement for them to annotate their pictures, can be very useful.

The organization of the children's ideas into three groups does provide a manageable basis on which to plan for the provision of teaching. The child in the first 'group' probably needs further experience of sound makers, and discussion with the teacher about sound having a source. The children in the second group seemed to have understood that sound comes from somewhere. These children probably need to explore and experience sound travelling, by listening to it under water, as it travels along wood (table tops) etc. and through string telephones. In this way they might come to understand that sound does not come from somewhere and bathe the area in sound. The last group have an understanding that sound has a source and that it travels, but they need to explore a little further in order to understand that sound travels in all directions at once. It might simply be a case

Figure 3.10   Representing sound: indication of a source, but not of sound travelling

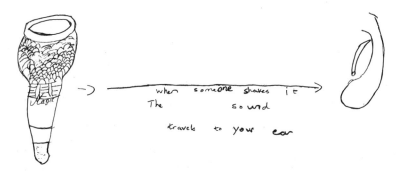

Figure 3.11   Representing sound: indication of a source, and of sound travelling to the hearer

of pointing out to the group in discussion that several people at a time can hear the same sound, or that a bell can be heard no matter where you stand around it.

Ideas about soil formation (analysing children talking)

The children from a school in a town by the sea were taken to a beach they were familiar with. The intention of the visit was to study how soil is formed. The children knew the area well, many rode their bikes down the long path to the beach regularly. On the long walk through the dunes to the beach the teacher discussed the plants growing in the area with the children, focusing on the medium they grow in and how they got there.

Teacher: Have you seen the heather there on the Heath?
Garry: Yes, it comes out all flowers later.
Teacher: How do you think it got there?
Garry: It got planted.
Nikita: It comes from Scotland.
Teacher: What would there be if the heather hadn't got there?
Jan: Nothing Miss, just bare.
Teacher: Can plants only get there if people plant them?
Garry: Yes Miss, or they could come from seeds that have blown.
Jan: Yes, weeds are always in the soil.
Teacher: How do they get there?
Jan: The cases in the soil are there and when you plant a plant the roots of it grow out and touch the case and that lets the weed grow.
Teacher: So, you don't think weeds can grow without people?
Jan: No, you have to plant something.
Garry: I think weeds grow for themselves when they land in soil.
Teacher: Does it have to be soil?
Nikita: Yes it does, plants need soil.
Teacher: What's under the heather?
Garry: Soil.
Teacher: How do you think the soil got there?
Jan: It's always been there.
Teacher: What is soil made of?
Garry: It's just soil and seeds, and sometimes round here

it's got some sand mixed in because it blows in from the sea.

Teacher: Well, where do you think the sand came from?

Jan: It comes from the sea, it gets dry then it blows about.

Teacher: But where did the sand come from before that?

Nikita: Rocks, Miss.

Teacher: How?

Nikita: The sea rubs bits off the rocks and they make sand.

Garry: It comes from wearing down stones too.

Jan: That's right you get sand from stones.

Teacher: Where do the stones come from?

Jan: They come along in lorries and some of them fall off.

The three pupils had different ideas about what plants can grow on and how they get there. One child believed seeds could be planted without human intervention, while the other two thought people needed to plant things. During the morning the teacher found this to be a common idea among the children in the group. They all felt that plants could not grow in sand alone, that there had to be soil. Yet they were familiar with marram grass. As children revealed their ideas the teacher directed them to look carefully at the 'soil' under the heather, or where the marram grass was growing. She also talked to the rangers for the area, who guided the children back through the dunes. The rangers were aware that the children thought everything was planted by people – which is close to the truth in this area, as it has been managed for over a hundred years. The rangers had also been asked to describe the gradual formation of dunes, and then the colonization of the dunes by different species of plants.

At the end of the day one of the pupils sought out the teacher.

Garry: Miss, I've found out about the heather place, it used to be dune.

Teacher: Really, all the way up here?

Garry: Yes, but it got plants growing on it and turned it into flat heath land.

Teacher: So, is it sand under the heather?

Garry: Yes it is, it got to be soil.

Teacher: How do you think that happened?

Garry: Soil got mixed in with the sand and bits of leaves and twigs.

Teacher: Well, thanks for telling me, how did you find out?
Garry: It's a bit in my workbook, so I asked the ranger.

These extended excerpts are intended to demonstrate that when a teacher has a clear idea about what it is she or he wants to teach, the questions asked of the children can be very focused and will reveal the ideas held by the children to the teacher, and also to the child.

Other strategies

The three strategies described above, using children's drawings and writings and listening to them talk, do not represent all possibilities. Other ways to find out children's ideas have been suggested and are fairly widely used. Teachers need a wide repertoire of such techniques in order to select the one that is most likely to provide best opportunity for the children to explore and develop their ideas. Caravita and Hallden (1994: 100) provide a charming explanation of why the selection of appropriate strategies is so important:

> We also think that productive pathways for teaching should take advantage of the resources that children use to make sense of the life of the body instead of focusing on what is lacking in the children's understanding. By resources we mean the personal 'treasure chest' of kinaesthetic sensations and of unvoiced observations about themselves, the others, the animals and plants that everyone collects since the beginning of his/her life.

One example Caravita and Hallden give is of asking children to construct a model of what they think is inside a rabbit using bits and pieces to stand for the different parts of the rabbit. They observed that the children included far more organs and connections between organs than they would have done had they been asked to talk about what a rabbit is made of, or to draw it. Modelling is a powerful tool for helping children to explore their own ideas and for encouraging them to make their ideas explicit. Concept maps (Harlen *et al.* 1990; Sorsby *et al.* 1992) and group discussion have not been discussed here, yet they represent strategies that many teachers find useful. In the following section I want to discuss the various approaches to planning in relation to the different ideas children have.

Using starting points: some models

Grouping children according to their initial ideas

In the above discussion I have outlined how when all members of a class of children can express their ideas differently it is possible to identify a limited number of groups based on the concepts the teacher wants to promote. I have also suggested ways in which planning might be based on the groupings identified. This is one way to proceed. Crossley (1991) found out the ideas held by her class of 7 and 8 year olds by asking them to record their ideas about a car travelling down a slope. She then identified four groups of ideas related to forces (the topic the class were embarking on), and grouped the children accordingly. The different groups then carried out some investigations around questions arising from their initial ideas.

Group 1   Idea: the wheels make it move.
           Question: do all things which move down the ramp have wheels?
Group 2   Idea: the slope makes it move.
           Question: what is needed to make a car move on a flat surface?
Group 3   Idea: it moves because the slope is slippy.
           Question: what effect do different surfaces on the ramp have on how the car moves?
Group 4   Idea: gravity makes it move.
           Question: what effect does raising or lowering the ramp have on the car?

The strategy adopted allowed the children the opportunity to explore their own ideas practically. Crossley points out that this approach was just as effective with the less able children in the class, because their work was based on their ideas rather than on reading and writing ability.

In another case a teacher of 9 and 10 year old pupils was undertaking a topic on human reproduction and linking this to ideas about inheritance and variation. The ideas the children held initially were gathered using a variety of activities. This was because the teacher was involved in a research project looking at progression in the National Curriculum for science (Russell *et al.* 1994). The children were given a range of tasks. One asked them to make a series of drawings to show where a baby develops from. Another asked them to make a prediction as to what some baby mice might look like, given drawings of their parents. Another asked them how, given two dogs with patchy coats, and offspring with patches of different sizes, they might breed a dog with a single colour coat. This last task was extremely demanding and required an understanding of the mechanisms of genetics.

The teacher used all this information to group the children into two basic groups. One group included children who had some understanding of the mechanisms of inheritance. These also included children who showed knowledge of how a baby develops, knowing that information in the sperm and egg is contributed from both parents. These children had explained inheritance in terms of the passing down of information from parents. In some cases they had used the word gene, but in other cases they had used a word in a very specific way: 'They got their *look* from their parents.' The second and largest group in the class had demonstrated a good deal of confusion about how information is passed from generation to generation. Many also had only a sketchy idea about the process of reproduction in humans.

The teacher adopted a mixed methodology in her approach to classroom organization. This allowed her to work closely with one group, those with some idea about reproduction and inheritance, while the other groups were doing different, non-science activities. The following are some excerpts from classroom observation notes.

A group of eight children sat round a long narrow desk (this made it very difficult for whole-group discussion)

Teacher: We talked about species before. What do you think a species is?
Jonothan: Same kind of animal but different.
Teacher: Can you give me an example?
Jonothan: There are lots of kinds of ants but they could be different kinds.
Teacher: Now, I want you to look at the pictures. And to think about them, are they all the same?

The teacher gives out some books open at particular pages, one book per pair. One has a picture of zebras, one of wasps, one of flowers and one of butterflies.

Marie: They are all just a teeny bit different.

The teacher leaves this group to go and work with another group.

Jonothan: Colour differences.
Aisha: They are not all completely blue
Teacher: They aren't all completely blue are they? Look at the patterning around the edges.
Aisha: That's browny orange and that's a blue red. It could have something to do with old and young. They could lose their red as they get older.
Simon: Some lines are quite faint.
Melisa: Some are thin.
Teacher: Why is it that there are differences?
Susan: Their mum might confuse them all. Then the mum might have some spots and the dad might have loads of spots.
James: She is thinking about the dogs.

In this small snippet of a lesson, the children focused on were making links between their observations and other experiences: their own experience of people changing as they get older or all having different faces, and the activity concerning selective breeding in dogs they had been given in the previous week. The teacher's intention in setting this task was to point out to the children that variation occurs within all species. Further discussion in this group quickly got on to the idea of inherited characteristics. With some encouragement the children decided to explore the notion of the inheritance of characteristics by looking at their own family trees. They suggested looking at eye colour, hair colour and type etc. This group quickly moved into discussions about the inheritance of characteristics from their parents and grandparents, and discussed the similarities between themselves and their cousins. They were clearly able to draw on their own observations and make connections between this and the methods by which characteristics might be inherited.

The rest of the class were not introduced to the activity described above immediately. Instead the whole class was introduced to the topic of human reproduction. The school nurse came along and showed a film, and discussed issues related to health and relationships with the children. The video explained about sperm and egg and how a baby develops. Only after this activity did the teacher again work with groups to discuss the idea of inherited characteristics. The groups who had not initially demonstrated any understanding of the inheritance of characteristics were able to use their new biological knowledge as a basis for a consideration of the inheritance of characteristics. They were then in a position to design the researching of their family trees.

The children who came to the topic with little insight into the idea of variation were able to deduce from their family tree work and their work on reproduction that there must be a mechanism for inheritance. One child initially held some very unusual views about how he came to look as he does:

> when they pop out it's a surprise, because if your dad's talking like my dad was; I grew up to be like my Dad, for some reason ... And when we visited again to have my brother taken out, he didn't talk at all, so he grew up looking like my Mum, for some reason.
>
> (Russell *et al.* 1994: 45)

The explanations given were not entirely satisfactory for the child, as is apparent from his use of 'for some reason'. However, after the topic he was thrilled with his new knowledge: 'There were genes in the sperm and genes in the egg, and I got more genes from my dad and my brother got more from my mum' (Russell *et al.* 1994: 47).

Towards the end of the topic the teacher felt that the group of children who had been clearer about the mechanisms for the inheritance of characteristics might benefit from further work in this area, leading them to an understanding of genes. She decided that to do this she needed to introduce them to the idea that living things are made up of cells within which the hereditary information is carried.

> This is what I found when I got my children, looking up on genes and the information, because we had done genes in health. They had got the egg and the sperm and the information passed on, family trees. And they had traced back various inherited characteristics, and we had sort of homed back in on the egg and the sperm, that sort of thing. And then I wanted to take them into cells and we had the microscopes out and we got the onions out and we looked at cells through that. But I found that they were more interested in

using the microscopes to look at other things. You know I
think I met a sort of block with that.

The children in this class needed to spend some time exploring
the microscope before they could move on to thinking about
cells. Only then would they be ready to return to the ideas of
genetics and take on board the idea of chromosomes and genes.

In the example detailed above the teacher grouped the children into two according to their ideas. The activities undertaken
by the two groups were ostensibly the same, although they occurred in a different order. However, the teacher's own input, in
terms of the questions she asked and the demands she made on
the groups, were different.

The grouping of children according to their initial ideas is not
something I have observed happening in many classrooms. There
are many reasons for this, including the general approach to
classroom organization adopted by the class teacher. However,
this kind of grouping may be appropriate in some circumstances,
so it is worth experimenting with, and adding to the repertoire
of strategies available.

Setting up open-ended activities

The extended description of the work of Jeanette Crossley above
is given because it links children's ideas, practical exploratory
activity and differentiation. Many teachers of primary science,
particularly in the early years, are concerned to ensure that the
science they do with their pupils encourages curiosity and helps
to develop the process skills of science. Much emphasis was placed
in recent years on developing children's ability to raise questions
and find ways to answer them. Jelly (1985) focused on the difference between: productive questions, which promote science as a
way of learning, and lead to first hand explorations to find answers; and unproductive questions, which lead to the gathering
of facts and seem to reflect a view of science as immutable knowledge. I would argue that a productive question for a learner is
one that leads to the seeking of solutions that develop understanding. This can only be done if the questions raised arise out
of ideas held by individuals. Questions cannot be raised in a
vacuum.

Children need a reason for raising questions. Some years ago the APU science team were looking at children's performance in investigations with giant African land snails. They explored the kinds of questions children raised when presented with these fascinating creatures. Many of the questions were not easily testable: 'Where does it come from?' 'Are those its eyes on the end of its tentacles?' 'What is that slime trail?' 'Did you get it from the zoo?' These are 'non-productive' questions in the sense that they would not lead to an experiment, but they are of interest to the child. They could lead to the child seeking out answers to questions using books and other secondary sources. Other questions are investigable: 'What does it eat?' 'Does it like to live in the warm or the cold?' The approach children might take to answering these questions would depend, in part, on what they already knew about animals, and indeed what they knew about Africa. The use of secondary sources, when the questions arise from a genuine interest on the part of the child, is a valuable way to find answers. Equally, the investigation of questions that arise from the interest and ideas of the child is a valuable way to find answers.

A Year 2 (6 and 7 year olds) teacher had been working with her class on the topic 'air'. The children had undertaken a number of investigations. They had, for example, built and tested land yachts and explored parachutes. They were therefore developing their investigative skills to quite a high degree for such young children. The next short topic involved working with sound and music. The children had worked on this topic in a previous class. The intention was to move them on a little, to complete the programme of study (the outline of content specified in the National Curriculum) for the key stage. The teacher worked an integrated day and had organized the children in the class into broad ability groups and decided to work with one group at a time, beginning with work looking at string telephones.

On a small easel Sue had written 'Our Question' in a cloud with question marks around it. On the floor stretched across the back of the room were four string telephones. One had large cups on the ends, one had green string and the others white, one was a little shorter than the others. Sue told the children that they were going to try to find some things out about the string telephone. She said that they would be talking to one another through the telephones. Two children were asked to have a try. 'I hear him.' The child looked into the cup and then put his finger into it to indicate that he could feel the vibrations. The second pair had a turn, speaking normally into the phone. 'I heard a banging in my ear.' The children all sat down again and the teacher asked, 'What was happening do you think?'

Robert: It was pressing through the string, gaps.

Teacher: Little gaps in the string?

Hayley: When we said something the sound bounces along the string. [Indicates with hand.]

Louis: I thought I saw a bit of electric going along the string.

Teacher: Louis thought he saw the string moving.

Robert: I thought it was following along the string.

The teacher asked him to explain that.

Robert: Along besides it, not in it – on both sides.

The ideas kept coming but began to get a little repetitive as the children tried to refine their ideas. The teacher began to write these ideas down.

John: There is a crack in the bottom of the cup and the voice gets out.

Teacher: How could you test it?

John: Try a thin gap and a bigger gap and see if it gets through.

Teacher: Alex, you haven't said anything.

Alex: It went out along the string and bounced.

Claire: It goes along the gap.

John: We could try a metal cup. If you speak into a metal cup it will be better because if you tap it it. [Shows vibration with hand.]

In this group of children the ideas about what tests to undertake were arising because they were being encouraged to think about why they could hear one another along a string telephone. The teacher allowed plenty of time for these discussions. The ideas presented were almost too many for her to record. However, as the discussion progressed she began to ask children how they would test their ideas. Suggestions rained thick and fast. The teacher then began to put the children into pairs, linking children with similar ideas. Where their ideas did not coincide she asked two children to work together to test out each suggestion.

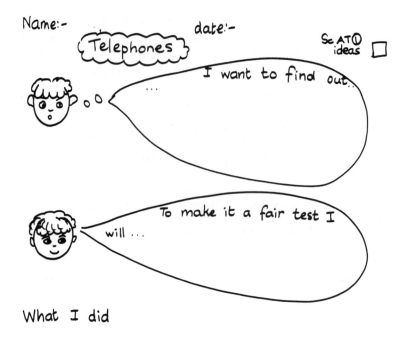

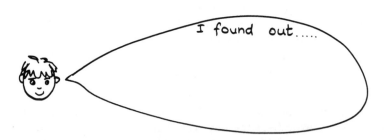

Figure 3.12 Testing string telephones

For example, one child thought that the presence of knots in the string would reduce sound transmission, while another was sure that the size of the hole in the bottom of the cup was crucial. They worked on both questions. All the children in the group used the same record sheet to record their work (see Figure 3.12).

The second group were not considered to be quite as able as the first. The teacher started by setting them a problem to find out if the telephones worked best with the string tight or with it loose. She did this because she felt that they would not get the most from the investigations if this was not explicitly pointed out to them. They were asked to investigate this question and record their findings on a sheet provided (see Figure 3.13).

The group moved on to the brainstorming session, where the teacher took a similar approach to that taken previously. However, the children did not express as many ideas about sound and were not therefore in a position to raise lots of questions.

Teacher: Where do you think the sound was going?
Ravinder: Because the string isn't in a big knot.
Teacher: How did it get from one cup to your ear?
Ravinder: When the knot moved the sound got out from underneath it.
Teacher: Where do you think the sound was going?
 . . .
Teacher: Do you think the sound can travel?
Pupils: Yes? Yes?
Ravinder: I want to test a tin telephone.
Teacher: Why?
Ravinder: Because that would be best . . . because it's bigger, it goes on your mouth.
Lauren: If the plastic is better.
Gerrard: Which one of the telephones we have is the best.
Faizan: Plastic is better.

Lauren and Faizan were encouraged to find out which type of cup was better, while Ravinder and Gerrard were asked to find out which type of telephone was the best. However, from the reactions of the children, the teacher felt that most of the group were not yet at a point where they could design an investigation. She encouraged this group to try out a number of string telephone activities, and followed this up with work on sound makers and experiencing sound travelling through different mediums.

The lessons described above were practically based science, but the basis on which investigative work was built was the pupils' own understanding. The teacher was able, through discussion, to help children to devise investigations that would test out their own ideas. She was also able, through the same process, to explore

Figure 3.13   Which is better?

their ideas so that suitable activities could be developed. Other groups in the class were started on activities in which they explored sound and sound makers, before moving on to higher level work.

Here the point is that where the children have some ideas on which to base their questions (the first group) they are able to raise investigable questions. However, where they have not developed a firm understanding of the concepts, they need further experiences (in this case of sound travelling etc.) on which to develop understanding. Knowing the point at which children would be in a position to devise investigations requires the teacher to listen intently to the children as they discuss their ideas. The teacher also needs to have a clear understanding of the concepts he or she wants to help the children develop.

Using children's ideas in discussion

It is clear that children will come to a topic with a wide variety of ideas. The discussion of these ideas can provide a useful basis for group or whole-class work. The following excerpt is from a teacher's discussion with a mixed-age class of 7 to 8 year olds about day and night and year length. Several weeks earlier the children had been asked to make drawings of their ideas. They were all sitting in a circle on the floor. The teacher had a large ball hanging from the ceiling, to represent the sun, and a hoopla hoop, with an 'earth' hanging from it, to move around the sun. He had the children's drawings to hand to help discussion.

Teacher: OK, let's talk about something else. I asked you to pretend you were in a space rocket coming back to earth. Can you remember your ideas about what you would see?

Helen: I saw some flowers and houses.

Teacher: Yes, you drew a village. What did other people draw?

Glen: My first idea was the sun moves.

Teacher: Where was it moving to?

Glen: The sun goes round the equator.

Teacher: Graham had a different idea. Tell 'em about your picture [handing him his original picture].

Graham: The moon is moving round the sun. [Asked to show

on the model, letting his finger be the moon, the child shows the moon in orbit round the sun.]

Teacher: What about the Earth?

Graham: It turns round as well.

Dean: The Earth moves round and spins, the moon stays in the same place.

Teacher: Anybody got any different ideas? Kerry, John, help me.

Helen: The Earth spins round and it also goes round the sun at some time.

Greg: The moon stays in the same place.

Teacher: Natalie's first idea was that the sun turns into the moon at night.

Ben: One side it's the moon and one side it's the sun.

Teacher: Do you still keep that idea?

Ben: No, I think it's dud.

Teacher: What made you change?

Ben: I learned something.

Teacher: OK, everybody give yourself a shake. [Class stand up and shake about for a minute.]

Teacher: Now, I am going to tell you what people have seen from space. You might have to change your own ideas a bit. [The teacher then begins to turn the globe.] What is the earth doing?

Pupils: Day / night.

The teacher then gets a child volunteer to control the overhead projector, so that it turns to face him as he 'orbits' the sun.

Teacher: Does the sun only shine on one place? [Discussion of the limitations of the OHP as a model of the sun.]

The teacher turns the Earth.

Teacher: Now, what is it like for Samantha? [Samantha is a card cut-out person standing on the model Earth.]

Pupils respond with 'day, night, day...' As he turns the Earth the teacher walks all round the circle (the Earth orbits the sun).

Teacher: How many days does it take?

Glen: One week.

Simon: Two weeks

Glyn: One year.

Teacher: How many turns?

Pupils: 365.

Teacher: It goes round about 365 times. If one spin equals one day and 365 spins is one year, how many days to go round the sun?

The children do not answer so the teacher says that 365 days equal one year. Year length is a new idea that the children are uncertain of. The teacher decided to take time to discuss the idea with the children further.

The teacher in the excerpt made it explicit to the children that they were to re-examine their own ideas in the light of new evidence. Thus whole-class teaching, in circumstances where children feel comfortable enough to express their ideas, can be a valuable approach that allows the exchange of ideas so that children can learn from one another. A teacher of 10 and 11 year olds mentioned that he had some difficulty in setting up this kind of open discussion with his class, because, by that age, many children feel reluctant to reveal their ideas in case they are wrong. That teacher opened the discussion by telling the class what he had thought made day and night when he was younger. He told them he thought God drew the curtains in the sky. The children laughed and started to challenge this idea: 'Well, how can you see the stars then?' The teacher said that the curtain had tiny holes in for light to get through. 'What about rockets going up?' The teacher thought that perhaps God drew the curtain back a little for them to get through. The children were pitting their ideas against those of the teacher. Class and group discussions can be extremely useful in helping to promote understanding.

So where do we start?

There are many other ways in which children's initial ideas can be explored and many strategies that a teacher might use to structure lessons so that initial ideas provide a starting point. The selection of different approaches is determined by a great many factors. A topic on the planets does not lend itself to open-ended investigative work, so this clearly does not provide a starting point, whereas a topic on light might start with lots of little activities to encourage children to think about their initial ideas. The selection of appropriate strategies is not only determined by the nature of the topic to be studied. Teachers will select an approach that will fire the children's interest and encourage all the children in the class to ask questions, to explore ideas and to want to know more. One of the most rewarding kinds of feedback I ever receive from children is when a child has spotted something at home or on television, or has brought something into school that shows that he or she has been motivated enough to carry on learning outside the classroom. The selection of approaches to teaching a topic must take into account all sorts of things about the children in the class, and the community from which they come. It is this aspect of individual differences and similarities that I address in the next chapter.

4

Factors influencing
children's science

Introduction

In Chapter 3 I looked specifically at children's ideas as starting points for learning. Without some idea of children's ideas a
teacher cannot begin to plan. Yet simply knowing their ideas is
not enough. If it were, differentiation would not be so difficult
to achieve. We need to go back to the idea of the whole child.
A child does not simply bring his or her own ideas to school;
he or she brings a culture, attitudes to school, to teachers and to
learning, ways of using language, learning styles, more or less
well developed motor skills and much more. All of this can make
the classroom a lively, exciting, sometimes daunting, place to be
for a child. And it makes the job of the teacher very demanding.
It is this huge variety of issues with which the teacher must
engage that turns teaching from a science into an art. I do not
believe that there can be any formula for planning the provision
of differentiated learning experiences. But I am sure that, unless
a teacher has insights into the ways in which different factors

influence a child's learning, he or she will miss so much, and will make so many assumptions. In this chapter I am attempting to cover a wide area, but essentially the message is a simple one. Teachers need to get to know and to keep on getting to know the children they teach. This is the only way a teacher can provide equality of access for all children to the curriculum.This is one aspiration expressed for the National Curriculum:

- The principle that each pupil should have a broad and balanced curriculum which is also relevant to his or her particular needs.
- That principle must be reflected in the curriculum of every pupil. It is not enough for such a curriculum to be offered by the school; it must be fully taken up by each individual pupil (NCC 1989).

The case of gender

Research into the relationship between gender and science learning has been undertaken in many countries for some time. Science is seen as a masculine subject. Most scientists are men, and most jobs that are perceived as requiring a high degree of scientific literacy are held by men. Children see this and reflect it when asked to describe a scientist, or identify jobs that are appropriate for males and females (Scholfield *et al*. 1989: Chapter 3). When asked to draw a scientist, many children draw a scatty looking, white, often balding man in a white coat mixing potions in a lab full of strange equipment (Newton and Newton 1991). Children get these ideas from the television and films, where stereotypical scientists are presented. Even postgraduate teacher training students with a science degree draw a similar scientist. Of course, it is true that many scientists are men, but it does not mean that they have to be men.

The evidence suggests that young children do not see the science that they do in school as the domain of the boys. Many girls as well as boys enjoy science in the primary school. It is also true, in England and in many other countries (Parker and Offer 1987), that over recent years since the introduction of science for all throughout compulsory schooling, girls perform as well as boys, or better in science exams at 16 (see Table 4.1). The introduction

Table 4.1 1994 science exam results for students in England (15 and 18 year olds)

	No. of boys	No. of girls	Boys points[a]	Girls points[a]
GCSE biology	9265	5441	5.37	5.39
GCSE chemistry	9193	5177	4.82	4.65
GCSE physics	9328	5139	5.56	5.24
GCSE combined science, single award	27,025	30,305	3.21	3.40
GCSE combined, dual award	185,806	183,109	4.43	4.39
Advanced level biology	7836	12,399	24.2	26.7
Advanced level chemistry	9704	7083	32.2	30.6
Advanced level physics	12,301	3116	30.8	28.1

GCSE is taken at the end of compulsory schooling (age 15–16); advanced level is taken after a two-year course of study (age 18).
[a] GCSE grades are scored A = 8 points to G = 1 one point. Average points are calculated for boys and girls. Pecentages of students achieving grades C or above are given for A level results.
Source: OFSTED (1995: Annex A).

of science throughout compulsory schooling is a necessary, but not sufficient, requirement for more girls to follow a career in science, or even to study it beyond compulsory school age. As Table 4.1 indicates, the tendency is for the more able pupil intent on specializing in the sciences to take the three separate science subjects. This is reflected in the higher average points scored. It is noteworthy that far fewer girls take this route. This figure is balanced by the larger number of girls taking combined single science and achieving higher scores than the boys. A larger proportion of more able girls are taking single awards than more able boys. The problem is that, as they move into adolesence, it seems that children's stereotypical views become greater (Jannikos 1995). Their views are often quite justified when they look at science and scientists, and are often supported by parents and teachers. Hendly *et al.* (1995) studied the attitudes of boys and girls to a range of subjects at the end of Key Stage 3 (age 14).

They found that boys had more positive attitudes towards science, technology and mathematics than girls. Girls had a more positive attitude to reading and writing in science than boys. So, despite catching up in the end of compulsory schooling exams, girls are not choosing to take science on once it stops being compulsory. Table 4.1 shows that girls are less likely to take advanced level physical sciences than boys, while more take biology than do boys.

What are the implications of this information for primary teachers, particularly when both the boys and the girls in the class enjoy science? To answer this we need to ask several questions. Do they enjoy and learn from the same sorts of things in science? Do they have equal access to the science activities presented to them? Can we leave it until the secondary school to address the issue of girls and science with them? These questions arise from the research on gender and science education. There has been much less work done on the relationship between culture and science education. However, the evidence indicates that some of the same issues apply to questions concerning science education and ethnic or cultural differences. During the following discussion I will pick up on these issues where appropriate.

What interests girls and boys in science?

When we look around any class of 4 and 5 year olds we can see differences straight away between the boys and the girls. They dress differently. Often they have different ways of behaving. This is because, from the beginning, they are treated differently. It is not difficult to see how these differences emerge. Clearly children are treated differently from an early age because of their sex, although people are often quite unaware of this. Naima Browne and Pauline France (1985) looked at the different ways in which boys and girls were described in a nursery class. They found that a girl who was quiet, withdrawn and diffident with adults was described as shy, while a boy was described as the strong silent type. A girl who organized others and initiated activities was described as bossy, while a boy would be hailed as a born leader. Enlightened teachers and parents make efforts to 'treat them all the same'. However, there are so many factors within society that treat them differently that we are often driven to believing that there are some inherent differences between boys and girls. Of course there are, but these are unlikely to be differences that make it more difficult for one group or another to play with the big blocks. Yet often the boys head for these toys and other construction kits, while girls play elsewhere.

Murphy (1994) reports that boys' and girls' performance on assessment activities designed to test ability to use measuring instruments was equal, except in relation to the use of instruments such as ammeters, stop clocks, force meters, hand lenses and voltmeters, where boys did better than girls. These instruments were the very ones that boys, but not girls, reported having experience of in their everyday life. They are perhaps more likely to have helped with mechanical or electrical jobs around the house, or to have used electrical toys more than girls. This means that boys tend to feel more confident with equipment when it is presented to them than do girls. There has been much speculation and some research into the effects of early tinkering activities on later performance in science. Kelly (1987) argues that performance in science at the ages of 11 and above is only slightly influenced by earlier tinkering activity. It seems that it is not girls' ability to do science that is in question, but their interest in it and their continuing enthusiasm for it.

As a parent I felt I made every effort to provide my daughter with a full range of toys, dolls, cars and construction toys. She never played much with dolls, but nor did she take to the construction toys or the cars. A friend gave her daughter a toy tool kit for a present. The child was later found rocking the screwdriver to sleep. It is not enough to treat children the same. Friends and grandparents showed my son how to play with cars by playing with him. No one not even I, showed my daughter how to play with the trucks we gave her. This sounds like a trivial point, but it is commonly noted that girls, when given a context where a real human problem needs to be solved, will engage readily with construction toys and can become very involved in design and technology (Grant and Givens 1984). Once the girls have a way into the knowledge involved, they quickly develop their skills. Boys are more likely to know how to manipulate things like construction toys, and so are more easily able to see their potential. This suggests that girls and boys engage with different problems because they are concerned with different issues. This provides a clue as to the different reactions girls and boys might have to different science activities they are presented with.

The APU in science surveyed the performance of English, Welsh and Northern Irish children at the ages of 11, 13 and 15 across many different science tasks. The intention of the programme was to provide information about standards of performance of the children of the country as a whole. Many questions were set in many different contexts, using a wide range of response modes. Not every child needed to try every question, as the project was not attempting to compare individuals or schools. This survey provided a wealth of information about the ways in which pupils reacted to questions. It provided information about not only who got what type of question right, but also what sort of errors different groups of pupils made.

Murphy (1989) discussed the gender differences observed in APU results. She described how, irrespective of what is being assessed, 'questions that involve such content as health, reproduction, nutrition and domestic situations are generally attempted by more girls than boys.' The girls also tended to achieve higher scores on these questions. In questions asking for the interpretation of graphs, for example, performance by girls was enhanced when the graph was of a secretary's day, while some boys simply did not answer this question. The situation was reversed when the question was about traffic flow through a town. Although these examples all arise from assessment questions, the implications for planning teaching are clear. Girls are more likely to engage with some tasks and boys others. McGarvey and his colleagues (1993) give a good example of this. The following is an excerpt from their report.

The class move slowly round the site looking and listening as Mr Brown explains what's happening. The site workers show the children the earth movers, diggers and grabbers in action and Mr Brown patiently answers the children's questions. The visit is a great success and the children glow with pleasure as Mr Brown thanks them for being so well behaved, well prepared, and knowledgeable.

Back in the classroom Mary quickly reviews the visit and explains she wants the children to record their experience. All the boys and some of the girls are keen to discuss the machinery and record their observations by drawing and writing. They are quickly organised into twos and begin work. However, nine of the girls protest and say that although they enjoyed the visit they find the machinery boring, and they don't want to sit and draw it. Mary has foreseen this problem and asks the girls to write a comic strip about a rabbit family's fight for survival as their field is turned into a housing development. The girls divide themselves into three groups and start planning their stories. They are anxious to make the stories as realistic as possible and start to collect books and leaflets which they look at as they discuss which machine will do what.

(McGarvey *et al.* 1993: 99–100)

In this example, the teacher had recognized the different levels of engagement with the task exhibited by some girls. She modified the task so that these girls' interest was engaged. This meant that they could access the skills and knowledge that they had. This example illustrates how, as with the assessment example mentioned by Murphy, the context affects how girls approach a task. It goes further, because the implications of such differentiated provision in planning are indicated. The method of reporting for the nine girls was a cartoon based on a story. The other children in the class gave responses of a more traditional nature. This affects the way the teacher can assess the children in the class. The girls themselves had been a part of the decision to change the context of the task. They could only do this in an environment where they felt comfortable enough to 'protest'. The nine girls worked in groups of three, but cooperated with one another, so a form of groupwork, different from the pairs working on the original task, was allowed. Moreover, the teacher had thought about the effect of the task set on different pupils in the class beforehand. I will discuss group organization later in this chapter; for now I want to concentrate on the effect of context.

The APU surveys were not restricted to assessment questions, as they included questionnaires exploring a variety of issues. These included the interests and experiences of pupils and their views of the importance of science as a subject for them. In one questionnire, 13 year old pupils were given a list of statements related to science and asked to indicate how interested they were in knowing more about each item (Qualter 1992). The items included 'how bald tyres increase the risk of car accidents', 'how plants and animals depend on each other' and 'how friction works'. As with the first and last examples, some statements were presented in terms of abstract concepts, with the same idea also being presented in terms of its application. The hypothesis was that girls would be more likely to find the application statements of interest and boys the abstract. It was also thought likely that girls would go for the biological and boys the physical. Nothing is ever that simple. The abstract type statements were of less interest to both boys and girls, although boys were not as negative about them. Girls were quite consistent in rejecting the abstract physical science statements. However, it emerged that girls do not simply select biological topics; rather they are interested in issues that they see as relevant to them and to the world. They were interested in 'how bald tyres increase the risk of car accidents' but not in 'how friction works'. Nor were boys interested only in the abstract, hard sciences: they too were interested in applications of science. Perhaps they are more tolerant of science, even when they don't see its immediate relevance, because they see it as a masculine subject that will get them a job (see Scholfield *et al.* 1989: Chapter 3). The results of the analysis of this questionnaire suggest that science that is portrayed as relevant to the needs of society and of the individual is of interest to both boys and girls.

Grant and Harding (1987) looked at the entries for the Design Council awards for schools. They noted that although the technical quality of the entries was as high for girls as for boys, the choice of problem and the description of the reasons for selecting particular problems were different. The majority of boys in the 1981 entries (53.5 per cent) tended to describe the technical challenge of their design problem. They were concerned with getting it to work better. All the girls described their problem in terms of the extent to which it met a human need. However, many of the boys' teams were also concerned with human need. There are therefore differences in general between the approaches boys and girls take to problems and in the interest they show in different aspects of problems. Despite these differences there is a large degree of overlap, which means that it is not possible to assume that, for example, because a child is a boy he will be motivated simply by the apparatus and getting it to work. He might be more likely to, but he is also likely to be motivated if he sees the relevance of the activity to him and to the world.

Are ethnic differences relevant to science learning?

In a recent research project, primary teachers across England were asked about their approach to dealing with gender and ethnic differences within their planning and teaching. Many teachers responded that they treat all children the same. Others, although only a few, mentioned the need to reflect children's own cultural and gender identity in their teaching (Russell *et al.* 1994). Research looking at teachers' assessment of pupils' abilities in high schools has shown that teachers tend to assign pupils from ethnic minorities to lower ability bands than performance on entry to the school would suggest (Wright 1987; Mortimore *et al.* 1988). In the early days of the development of standard tests for 7 year olds the three groups working on the test development explored the relationship between teachers' own assessments and the results of the standard tests. The tests were very different from the tests that are now used; indeed externally set tests in science for 7 year olds are no longer used. Teachers were less clear about how to interpret the requirements of the National Curriculum and its assessment. However, the lessons drawn from some of the data generated leave cause for concern. One group (NFER/BGC 1991) identified a trend for teachers to assess pupils from ethnic minorities lower than other pupils. This could be because, in the early years, teachers focus more on the development of English speaking and writing skills and so give less time to science where English is not the child's first language. However, another group found that children tended to do better on the test than their teacher's assessment would have predicted (CATS 1991). Although these data are based on very early work in this area, they do suggest that teachers themselves might be underestimating the potential achievements of pupils from ethnic minorities. Shorrocks *et al.* (1993) also found that in the first round of the Standard Tests for 7 year olds, teachers were assessing children whose first language was not English lower than monolingual children, and below the level at which they were assessed on the Standard Tests. I would suggest that, being in some ways a new subject, and one to which all children can contribute, no matter what their background, primary science ought to be an area in which teachers can successfully promote learning in all pupils. Yet the evidence is that some teachers do not treat children equitably.

Part of the problem is that science is seen as universal, or without any cultural values. It is hard to see that the science we generally present is Western in character. The scientists we mention to children, or those they see depicted in the media, are generally white as well as male. Children's drawings of scientists generally show white males working alone in a lab. When we think of the things around us that are the result of scientific advances we tend to think of high-tech machines, like the computer and spaceships. Third World countries are seen as backward, because these things are not available to most of the population. Yet science affects all our lives, wherever we come from. The development of appropriate technologies is just as much an intellectual challenge in one country as it is in another. Science teaching needs to demonstrate that science is for everyone. This does not simply mean ensuring that all children in a class do science, but also that the science they do is relevant to them, and that it addresses issues pertinent to them. The ASE working party on multicultural education discussed the role of science education:

> The Working Party believes that the issue of racism and access to the curriculum for all children in a multicultural society needs to be addressed as a matter of urgency. By its very nature, racism aims to devalue specific groups of human beings based on colour of skin and/or cultural and social background. If an entitlement to a balanced and relevant science curriculum (as, for example, stated in the National Curriculum for England and Wales) is to be taken up by every child, there must be recognition that in establishing equality of opportunity, racism will always have an effect on children's learning and achievement.
>
> (Thorp 1991: 171)

One way to promote the idea that science belongs to all is to include references to scientific discoveries, and to the way science was and is used by different societies, within the rest of the curriculum, as well as in science lessons. For example, when studying ancient Egyptians it is worth pointing out that even today's computers cannot compete with the design of the pyramids, and that, until the 1960s, Pharaoh Khufu's pyramid was the world's highest building. The Egyptians were great architects and they were black (they called themselves the Kemets, which means black people). Medical science has come a long way during this century, but even before this century the Ugandans were able to undertake caesarian sections, demonstrating that medical knowledge is by no means the prerogative of the European. Edison invented the light bulb. It took another (black) American scientist, Lewis Howard Latimer, to develop a light bulb that would last long enough for it to be useful (Forde *et al.* 1988). This kind of broadly based curriculum is valuable for all children and provides a basis for much discussion and debate. Information about Mary Seacole, a black nurse working in the Crimean War, is readily available in many history curriculum materials. Information about scientists past and present is less readily available. Yet getting to know the children in one's class also means ensuring that the curriculum provided does not exclude the experience of ethnic minorities. There are useful materials, but rarely from the mainstream publishers (see, for example, Peacock 1991 for information; see also Barnfield *et al.* 1991).

So far, I have focused on the notion of a multicultural approach to science teaching that is in its intent anti-racist. That is, the curriculum presented for children is such that it reflects and values the wide variety of cultural backgrounds from which people in our society come, and it challenges stereotypes, rather than ignores them. Obviously, most children from ethnic minorities in the UK were born in the UK, not Africa, the Caribbean or the Asian subcontinent. Thus, the children in any one class are likely to share a common culture in many respects. This means that a topic on a village in India, as part of the geography curriculum, does not in itself address the learning needs of Indian children in the class. Science in primary schools is practical and investigative. Troyna and Farrow (1991) argue that 'The very methodology by which we, as teachers, encourage the learning of science, is also the best vehicle for anti-racist education.'

What is needed is the ability on the part of the teacher to identify possibilities for starting points in science. Clayden and Peacock (1994) suggest that the teacher should begin by thinking about the context when choosing topics and materials. The topic 'ourselves' is a popular one, particularly with teachers of younger children. This topic provides plenty of opportunity to look at the homes, food, clothing, festivals and games and toys of different children. This topic can be broadened out to look at children from other parts of the world, but will start with the children in the class. There are traps we can all fall into. Clayden and Peacock (1994) provide a neat example of such a trap.

> A teacher once told me that he had carried out a survey with his class on 'What we ate for tea'. Being a multiethnic classroom, many children didn't have a clear concept of 'tea' or 'teatime', but they knew what 'English' kids had for tea, so they all wrote down 'fish and chips' or 'burgers', even though some were vegetarian.

In one multiethnic Year 2 classroom a teacher was embarking on a topic to look at similarities and differences between people. The teacher wanted the children to explore the idea that characteristics are passed down from one generation to the next. The teacher brought along a set of beautiful photographs of six children of different origins. She worked with a group of children discussing similarities and differences between the children in the photographs. She begins with 'I got these from the teacher centre. I liked them so much.' The children look at the pictures and discuss which ones they like best.

Teacher: Now, what I want you to do is to tell me any differences you can see between these children.
Leon: That one's different, it's a girl.
Peter: Girl.
Naime: Girl.
Kirsty: Boy.

The teacher picks up two photographs, of an East Asian child and an African child, and asks what is different about them.

Leon: They come from different countries, Iran.
Naime: Africa [pointing to the African child].
Kirsty: I didn't know.
Leon: She comes from China, she has Chinese writing [picking out one of the other pictures].
Teacher: But I could buy a jacket like that.
Kirsty: She has Chinese eyes.
Peter: There are two boys, she is a girl.
Leon: Different clothes.
Teacher: Yes. Carina, what do you think? [Carina shrugs.]
Naime: Pakistani or Indian.
Teacher: So this boy might be Indian, this boy might be African, what about the girl?

Carina: Her hair is like a girl's.
Teacher: Can you think of another difference?
Kirsty: He has lost two teeth.

The teacher recaps on the differences mentioned and asks why the African is different. The children say he is a different colour.

Naime: This one has a peachy face.
Zaffa: Kale.
Teacher: What does that mean? [Short exchange between Zaffa and Naime.]
Naime: Dark.
Teacher: So he is dark skinned. Carina, what differences can you see now we have two more? [Bringing all the photos into the line.]
Carina: Different colour hair.
Kirsty: Black eyes.
Teacher: Have they all got the same eyes?
Pupils: No.
Teacher: Zaffa, can you put them in two sets?

Zaffa separates the white, blonde girl into one set and keeps the others together. Then Zaffa and Naime make three sets, two with brown eyes, two with black eyes and one with green eyes.

Teacher: So we have sorted them for eye colour. What about hair?
Leon: You can't see his hair. [African boy has straw hat on.]

This excerpt shows the teacher encouraging the children to identify differences between the children in the photographs. She showed them that certain differences were not really a characteristic of the child (the jacket worn by one child), while others were. She also helped them come to an understanding that there are several ways in which people can be grouped according to their different characteristics. Where a child used a word from his home language, the teacher asked what it meant. Another child in the group who also spoke the language was able to help figure out a translation. Later in the discussion the children were asked to consider similarities. After some prompting they came up with lots of similarities between the children. This approach to an 'ourselves' topic did not start with a graph of eye colour or height, which is a common way to look at differences in a class of children. The teacher started by letting the children explore similarities and differences, so that they came to an understanding that some differences are relevant to the study of variation, while other are not. This approach does not ignore skin colour or facial features, but is positive about them. It is also important that the teacher went to some trouble to get good pictures of a variety of children – finding them in old magazines might have proven difficult.

Culture and scientific concepts

In earlier chapters I have suggested that children learn from their experiences both inside and outside school. It would follow that the language used at home as the child grows up, and the cultural environment in which he or she is raised, will have an influence on the ideas a child has. There has been very little research into this question. None of the major projects that have studied children's ideas have considered cultural differences, or for that matter gender differences, to any extent. There have been some international studies comparing children from different countries. Nussbaum (1985) and others (Mali and Howe 1979; Sneider and Pulos 1983) have looked at children's ideas about the Earth across a number of different countries. In general these studies found a similar progression in understanding for children in Israel, the USA and Nepal, although the Nepali children were slightly behind the others in the development of their ideas. In these studies the researchers compared children's ideas against a logical progression towards a scientific view. Differences might have been more easily detected had the children been given more open-ended questions about the nature of the Earth.

A group of teachers from Bolton, in a small-scale study, looked at children's understanding of the moon and its phases (Bolton Metropolitan Authority 1992). Some of the teachers involved had expected there to be cultural differences in how children understand the moon, because the moon and its phases play an important part in the pattern of some religions. No differences were detected between children from different ethnic minorities. Hanson, in a very small-scale study, looked at Nepali children's ideas about the processes of life (Hanson and Qualter 1995). When we compared the Nepali children's ideas with those gathered by the Primary SPACE project (Osborne *et al.* 1992), we found that the Nepali children seemed to have a better understanding of respiration than the children from the UK. The religious background of the Napali children who were involved in the study was mainly Buddhist. The beliefs of Buddhists about life and living things may account for the children's grasp of the notion that plants 'breathe'. George and Glasgow (1988), working in the Caribbean, looked at the interaction between everyday and school science explanations. They concluded that children from different cultural backgrounds holding different everyday ideas tended to develop different interpretations of school science explanations. This suggests that cultural background can make a difference to the meanings children make about the science experiences they are presented with in class.

In the studies reported above it might be argued that differences arise because children are speaking in different languages. Different languages might lead to differences in the concepts held by children. Lynch and Jones (1995) found that children from similar cultural backgrounds in the Philippines, but whose home languages were different, did exhibit some differences in the science concepts they held. These types of study are as yet too few to come to any conclusions. However, the fact that the differences, where noted, are small and may not have much impact in terms of ability to learn science suggests that cultural or linguistic differences between children in a class should not in themselves impede children in the development of their understanding of scientific concepts. That is not to say, of course, that learning science in a language other than one's home language is not going to pose an added burden, or that individuals will not gain particular concepts because of their experiences outside school. It therefore seems that, from the teacher's point of view, it is the importance of valuing the child and the child's cultural and ethnic background that is crucial. However, I will return to the issue of language and science learning later in this chapter.

Learning styles and group work

In recent years there has been something of a challenge mounted against the idea of group work in schools. Politicians and others associated with them have called for more whole-class teaching and an end to woolly minded notions of teaching. The pressure is for more formal teaching styles linked to a view of teaching as transmission and of learning as reception. It is not only the politicians who are concerned about group work. There have been reports by researchers that group work might not be the best way to promote learning. It is true that children often sit in groups while undertaking individual work, rather than working as a group (Bennet 1987), but this is not an argument against the efficacy of children working as a group. Galton (1995) discusses research relating pupil attainment to types of organization. The evidence suggests that, in general, whole-class teaching results in enhanced performance in English and mathematics. However, he concludes that it is not the style of organization that is the crucial factor, but the quality of teacher–pupil interactions. In whole-class teaching the teacher is able to ask more challenging questions. Organization based on individual assignments tend to leave the teacher with little time to do more than answer organizational or other low-level questions posed by children. Teachers who are able to arrange an individual work approach, so that they can ask intellectually demanding questions, are able to achieve similar levels of performance in their pupils as are gained through whole-class teaching. This seems to lean towards whole-class teaching, as it is easier to achieve a situation where challenging questions can be posed. However, Galton argues that collaborative group work is different again. This is an approach likely to be favoured in science teaching. It seems that if children are encouraged to be independent learners, rather than to ask for help all the time, they can make great gains from group work. Here group work involves genuinely working as a group, rather than sitting around the same table in a group and working alone. The issue is not which approach is best, but how best to encourage children to think things through for themselves. In science one of the principle aims is to encourage children to think scientifically. This can be done through discussion, between teacher and children and within groups.

In Chapter 3 I described a very exciting whole-class session on the Earth and space with a group of 7 and 8 year old children. The teacher asked challenging questions, and encouraged the children to puzzle out problems. He related the discussion to individuals' prior ideas. The children thoroughly enjoyed the session and, in interview some days later, they explained that they had learned a great deal from the topic. They said they had enjoyed it even more than the 'Tudors and Stuarts' topic running in parallel. However, a closer look at that teaching session (not all of which is reproduced in Chapter 3) reveals some interesting differences. The principal contributors to the discussion were boys. The teacher repeatedly asked individual girls to contribute: for example, 'Anybody got any different ideas? Kerry, help me.' Yet the boys jumped in and the girls did not.

> *Teacher*: Natalie's first idea was that the sun turns into the moon at night.
> *Ben*: One side it's the moon and one side it's the sun.
> *Teacher*: Do you still keep that idea?
> *Ben*: No, I think it's dud.

Ben answered for Natalie, even when the teacher asked her if she kept the idea. Here the teacher was aware of the lack of contribution by the girls in the class but was unable to draw them in fully. De Bóo and Farnell (1991) argue that it is not necessary to include all children in such exchanges. Children may not wish to contribute in such a way but may still be puzzling out their ideas. But by not opening their ideas up for discussion, these children are not getting the benefit of a fuller exploration of their ideas; nor are others in the class getting the benefit of hearing different ideas. This is an argument for a mixed approach to classroom organization, where different children have the opportunity to explore their ideas, perhaps in small groups or through writing or drawing. The phenomenon of the quiet child is observed not only in whole-class discussions but also in discussions with teachers in small group settings.

A Year 1 (5 year olds) class were working on magnets. The teacher had organized the children into groups. Most in the class were working on other activities and the teacher worked with one group at a time. The following are the notes I made based on my observations of the class.

The yellow group consisted of three boys and two girls. They were of average ability. Figure 4.1 shows the seating arrangement. The teacher began by showing the children four different magnets. They were quite different in shape and colour. Then she took up the large planning sheet and asked the children,

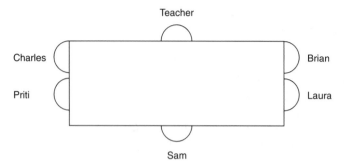

Figure 4.1   Seating plan for yellow group

'What do we want to find out?' This was the first box on the planning sheet. The children were clear about the aims of the work because this had been the focus of the class discussion previously. Charles replied, 'Which is the strongest magnet?' The teacher wrote this down in the box.

A discussion followed in which the children were encouraged to look at each magnet. They were then asked to think about how they thought they could find out which was the strongest. It was quite noticeable that two boys, Charles and Brian, did much of the talking, particularly Charles. The teacher asked them to think about what they might use to find out which was the strongest. The children (Charles first) quickly decided on how many pins each would pick up. They were asked to predict which magnet would be the strongest and to draw a picture of it.

The children made their predictions and then drew each magnet on a recording sheet so that they could record how many drawing pins each magnet picked up. The children took turns to try out a different magnet. Sam did not try a magnet. Each child counted the number of pins collected and drew them in the chart. Brian resented having to try the Alcan magnet, as he 'thought it would be the worst'. He did not want to be the loser. Charles picked this up and told him he lost (the teacher quickly intervened to insist that it was not a race).

The children recorded their results, and as a group counted the number of pins each magnet had picked up. Their teacher wrote the sum on the chart. The discussion that followed established the strongest magnet and the weakest (the Alcan one). The children seemed quite happy with their results, and could use 'stronger' and 'weaker' to describe the comparative strengths of each magnet.

During the group work the two girls, Priti and Laura, were exceptionally quiet. They hardly said a thing. They were obviously taking part in the work. They pointed to the magnet they thought was the strongest, and counted the number of pins their magnet had picked up. Charles and Brian tended to be very chatty and quick to answer, which may have made the girls less willing to say things. At the end of the lesson, when the children were on the carpet with the rest of the class, it was clear that the two girls knew the answers to the questions. The girls were whispering the answers to each other, but they did not once offer to answer to the whole class.

In the above excerpt four of the children were involved in the activity throughout. The two girls did talk to one another about the activity and answered the questions put to the whole class, but they whispered them to each other. Here the teacher might have attempted to draw ideas from the girls, so that their ideas could be shared with the group. Perhaps in this case the children needed to be taught how to work in a group, to become better able to share ideas and to gain from one another. One boy in the group was not contributing for different reasons. He had a very short attention span. The teacher explained that his parents thought he was hyperactive, a possibility that the school was looking into. The teacher was trying different ways of working with him. In this session the discussion and activity were controlled and mediated by the teacher. In part this was because she was attempting to teach the children how to work with the planning sheets that were being introduced to the class. It was the very start of a strategy by the teacher to develop in the children the ability to work as a group. Evidently further work needed to be done to encourage collaboration. Without this the children would continue to be dependent on her for learning to progress.

Horbury and Pears (1994) conducted a detailed exploration of young pupils' ability to work in collaboration. They demonstrated that children at Key Stage 1 (5–7 year olds) can develop the skills to work in this way. They concluded that children can manage the social dimensions of group work, and can approach a task in a cooperative way that enables them to progress successfully through the activity, without the continuous presence of the teacher. In a Danish study looking at boys' and girls' approaches to group work, Møller Anderson and Sørensen (1995) looked at groups of boys, groups of girls and mixed groups as they carried out science activities using Lego. They made video recordings and found that the girls tended to share the activity, each taking part in making the objects. While watching the video later, girls explained that they understood group work to mean the whole group sharing the task. Boys-only groups tended to work in a different way. One boy took the lead and the others acted as helpers, finding the Lego bits. They explained that they saw group work as the group getting the task done by dividing the labour. In mixed groups the boys tended to lead and the girls acted as helpers. The researchers used the opportunity of the video recordings to help the children evaluate their own working practices and to discuss approaches that might work better. This led to improved group work as the children began to recognize the need to share more. In another study, with Year 5 children, Rennie and Parker (1987) found that in classes where the teacher had an awareness of gender issues the children in the class were better able to work in mixed-sex groups. Otherwise, they found that it was better for the teacher to allow children to work in friendship groups, where they would cooperate more readily with each other. This is an important finding, as it demonstrates that teachers can reduce the effects of gender imbalance simply as a result of having explored the issues on a previous in-service course.

I am not advocating the abdication of the teacher from group work, but that by taking the time to help children learn independently teachers can free some of their time. It can also provide a learning environment that suits many children best, providing them with an opportunity to discuss and reflect on their own ideas and those of others. The focus above has been on raising the quality of the interactions between teachers and pupil. However, when children work as a group, independently, the interactions between children are crucial. Bennet and Cass (1989) describe a study of children working in groups of different kinds. They found that able children's learning was similar, no matter what kind of group composition they worked in. Less able and average ability children did not do so well in homogeneous groups. The most effective groupings were those where there was a mixture of pupils of a range of different abilities. This might explain why fewer teachers group children by ability in science than they do in subjects such as maths and English. An experienced teacher of mixed-age classes in a small primary school explained her use of mixed groups in science when she was asked how she copes with the spread of abilities.

> I don't cope with it by having all my high fliers together or all my low achievers together. The groups are mixed ability, because I feel that lends itself best to sharing of ideas. The less able, the less inspired are certainly able to benefit from the inspiration that the high fliers are able to give . . . I design tasks which can always be taken a step or two further by those more able pupils . . . For example, we did some work on acid rain and in the group they all tested substances for acid or alkalis. The ones who were able to go further than that and had got that part done and recorded, then they went on to actually using indicator strips and measuring acidity in different substances.
>
> (Teacher of children aged 8–11)

Setting up effective group work that supports all children as they learn is no simple operation. Because of the gender, ability and social skills of individuals, the development of effective, co-operative group work within a class is something a teacher needs to work at. It can be done, although it is essential to monitor the way groups are working and if necessary to change them to find the best mix. Children clearly need to develop the skills of working in groups, so that children of different abilities can work together and boys and girls can get the most out of the activities. It seems that this can best be done by discussion of the issues with the children, rather than an unexplained imposition by the teacher.

Is equal opportunity provided?

It is very difficult to evaluate one's own teaching dispassion-ately. However, this is something teachers need to do all the time. Research shows that teachers can unknowingly fail to pro-vide equality of opportunity for all children in their class. The Norwegian primary science project findings are of interest in this respect (Jorde and Lea 1987). During the project observations were made of teachers and pupils during normal science lessons. It was found that, in every class studied, irrespective of the sex of the teacher, boys received more attention than girls. They raised their hands and answered questions more often. They were called on to speak more. They were recognized as exhibiting negative behaviour more. Girls were quicker and better at writing up their activities, while boys tended to leap into practical work. Boys often went on to make up their own experiments once finished, instead of engaging with writing up. The researcher also found that teachers tended to encourage boys to find a solution to a problem, while they showed girls the answer. This last finding corresponds to observations of English high school practical lessons. Teachers were found to give verbal responses to boys' questions while they engaged in 'hands on' responses to girls' problems (Randall 1985). These findings suggest that teachers treat children differently. I have argued that it is appropriate to treat children differently because they have different needs, but the line between treating individuals differently and treating them inequitably is a fine one.

The issue of language

Language is crucial to learning in any subject area in school. Children need to be able to express themselves, and to understand the teacher as he or she talks to them. Further, from a very early age children are presented with the written word. Access to learning in science can be restricted for pupils who have not developed reading and writing skills at the same rate as their peers. This can be for many reasons, but whatever they are they can be a serious drawback to science learning unless the teacher can reduce the burden in some way. In one infant school (5–7 year olds) the teachers had decided to focus on the issue of differentiation over a whole school year. This involved in-service sessions, careful consideration of short- and medium-term planning by subject coordinators and a certain amount of experimentation in classroom practice to find strategies that were practicable. The school had made some headway, although staff were still rather baffled about differentiation in science. Yet the work on language and maths paid off in terms of the way one teacher of a mixed age class (6 and 7 year olds) structured her lessons. The session started with the teacher working with half the class on sound and sound makers. She wanted the group to discuss how sounds are made by different musical instruments. She encouraged children to talk about the musical instruments and the sounds they made, to come up in turn and, after making a prediction about how they would get sounds from the instrument, to try it out. There was a range of instruments from different cultures, with different ways of making a sound. The lesson showed a whole range of ways in which the teacher provided access to the topic by reducing the burden of language on the children.

During the session one non-English speaker had a language assistant in class with her. This teacher sat with the child during the discussion and translated, but she also asked her questions and explored her ideas. The language assistant did not see her role as simply translating the words of the teacher, but of engaging the child in thinking about the activity. The class teacher did not direct any questions towards this child, nor did the child come forward to look at the instruments, but she clearly enjoyed the session, communicating well with her helper. In this case access to the learning opportunity was provided by the language assistant.

During the lesson most children in the group had the opportunity to answer questions, and to try out different sound makers. One boy had problems keeping still (these were real difficulties, he was not just a fidget) and had as much as 80 per cent hearing loss. This was shown at one point, when one child explained that for a tambourine to be played it needed to be whacked. The boy heard this as wax, and commented 'wax is from candles'. The teacher picked this up, agreed that wax is in candles but corrected his error by repeating the first child's response with associated actions. During the whole session this boy sat at the front of the group, partly because as he wriggled and squirmed around he was likely to hurt another child by mistake. His attention needed to be kept by asking him questions, repeating or acting out the suggestions other children made and reminding him to try to keep still. This is very demanding of teacher time, but it ensured he took a full part in the work and was able to learn from it.

After much talk and lots of activity the children were set to work in groups. The teacher organized the groups by ability. The teacher first showed all the children a large poster she had made in which she had written the sound words the children would need to do their work. Alongside each word was a representation of the sound – so 'shake' had a picture of moving maracas next to it. The teacher pinned the poster to the wall, so that children could get out of their seats to go and look at it. This was intended to enhance visual memory of the words – an important facet in the development of spelling skills. One group of children immediately began to make use of this aid as they worked quite quickly and independently through their worksheet.

The worksheets were almost the same for each group. The children were given a set of pictures of instruments and asked to write down what they would have to do to make a sound. For some groups the appropriate words were given on the bottom of the worksheet; others could use the poster if they needed it. Most of the children worked with the sheet that had words written underneath the pictures. However, the teacher modified the activity as she moved around the class. One child did not begin his work until the teacher could give him some individual attention. She explained the task again and then she pointed out words and made the link between the worksheet and what they had been doing beforehand. One child had very few reading skills, and could not find the appropriate words on the page to write under each instrument. The teacher discussed each instrument with him and together they decided what the action was that made the sound. Then the teacher highlighted the appropriate word in one colour. She moved on to the next instrument and highlighted the action with a different colour, linking it through colour coding with the relevant instrument. This child could show his understanding of the science, but his lack of reading and writing skills meant that he could not do this on paper. The teacher worked with another child, sitting on the same table, but did not highlight the words in different colours. She talked about each one and pointed to and read the answers once the child had given the correct one. The child was then able to write the words into the appropriate space.

The lesson included a wide variety of strategies that the teacher used to provide access to the science. She kept the child who found it difficult to keep still near to her, keeping his attention by asking him lots of questions. The teacher helped him, and some of the children who were not fully bilingual, by linking actions to words; the child who spoke no English was supported by a good language assistant; strategies for spelling were provided; some children were given the opportunity to show their understanding through discussion rather than written evidence. Children were supported as they worked by the teacher, who accepted all responses and helped those who struggled with an explanation, but then rephrased responses so that other children could understand them. A great deal of differentiation was going on in this class, simply in relation to the language input, to give all children access to the science.

Language and the use of language is not simply a matter of access. The interactions between child and child and between teacher and child happen through language of one sort or another. Language has a crucial role to play in the development of children's concepts. 'The shaping of language is a means by which pupils reach deeper understanding of what is already partly grasped' (Barnes 1976). One of the most important ways in which children's conceptual development is promoted is through negotiation and discussion, where teachers use higher order questioning. McGuigan (1990) discussed the issue of teaching children the words associated with scientific ideas. She concluded that 'Merely supplying a child with a scientific label has not facilitated scientific understanding.' That is, for the development of scientific concepts language is not used merely to label things, but is used by the teacher, with the child, to negotiate meaning. This interaction between children and between children and teachers allows children to develop their spontaneous concepts (Piaget 1929) into more formal, non-spontaneous concepts. Walsh in Bentley and Watts (1994) discusses this through her observations of 7 year old children playing with toy boats. They are able to deal with the forces involved in floating and sinking, they can manipulate the boats so that they float or sink. They spend time talking about what they are doing and through this come to an understanding of why things sink.

> *Michael*: Look it's got six people and it's not sinking yet.
> *Hima*: I can make it sink. [She pushes it with her hand.]
> *Michael*: That's not fair, you pushed it down.
> *Penny*: I've used all my plasticine now and it's still floating.
> *Michael*: Well plasticine floats anyway, 'cos some of the people from my boat are floating on their own.
> *Hima*: No, they're not, they're sinking now, look. [She points to a person just beginning to sink.] It's too heavy.

Teacher: Could you try and make them float in the water, Hima?

Hima: No, they only float in the boat.

Michael: That one's floating.

Hima: No, it's not. [She pushes it gently with her finger but it still floats.]

Michael: See, it can't sink 'cos it's too big.

Penny: The bigger ones float but the smaller ones sink.

Michael: Yes, that's right.

Teacher: There is a very big lump of plasticine but look it's sunk to the bottom.

Michael: Oh yeah.

Penny: It's just a lump. [She fishes it out and squashes it flat on the table with her hand.] Now it'll float. [It floats.]

Hima: That's 'cos it's a boat now, you made it into a boat.

Teacher: Have you noticed the shape?

Michael: It's squashed and thin.

Hima: It's boat shaped.

Penny: It's just flat.

This excerpt shows how language is used to make the link between perceptions and experiences and concepts. It also shows the use of language to negotiate meaning. The children reached a deeper understanding of what they had already partly grasped. The implications of this for children who are not fluent English speakers are that the negotiated meaning might be lost and therefore the development of children's partly grasped concepts is not fulfilled. Often children who are at an early stage in learning English will be given labels for things, but this does not necessarily promote higher level understanding of concepts.

Cummins and Swain (1986) showed that bilingual children learn to speak English well, and do so more quickly where use of their home language is encouraged and supported. The evidence for the integration of home language into the approaches to teaching and learning adopted by the school is now difficult to dispute. It is likely that this has as much to do with the development of concepts through negotiation as it does with the ethos of valuing a child's background. This does lead to difficulties for the mono-lingual teacher with little support in a multilingual classroom. This is where close links with parents and the use of peer group tutoring pay dividends. As described above, a group of children working together can negotiate meaning and develop their conceptual understanding. Where some children in a group move into their home language to explore an idea they will benefit in terms of the development of their scientific understanding and their linguistic abilities in both languages. Again we return to the issue of group work. Carrington and Short (1989) argue for the wider use of collaborative or cooperative learning techniques that have been developed particularly in the USA (Slavin 1983). The arguments presented by Massey (1991) are for collaborative group work to address issues of race and cultural differences directly, but there is no reason why any other learning objective, such as developing scientific concepts, cannot also be promoted in this way.

Conclusion

This chapter has ranged over many issues. One area that I have not touched on is that of children with physical disabilities and science learning. Nor have I considered children who have statements of educational need because of behavioural difficulties. It is difficult in the space available to address all the issues. The problems involved in teaching children who are blind, for example, are not straightforward. It is not simply that they cannot see at the present time, but they have not had the opportunity to see in the past. Therefore blind children are deprived of the chance to develop certain concepts, or have more rudimentary concepts in certain areas than their sighted classmates. I can only say that an awareness of individuals' capabilities, their ideas and their difficulties is essential if learning opportunities are to be provided that children can make full use of.

In this chapter I have stressed the need for teachers to understand and value cultural and gender differences. I have also emphasized the need for collaborative classrooms, where pupils and teachers work towards a shared goal. We teach children in classes of over 20, and in recent years in classes of ever-increasing size. There are observations that can be made about particular sub groups of children (girls tend to . . . boys are likely to . . .), and this helps the teacher to plan and organize. But in the final analysis all children are individuals and need to be understood if they are to be able to make the most of the education that is offered to them. Primary science is an area that is rich in possibilities for all children. It provides a context for looking at people, for addressing gender and race issues, for looking at the world from many angles. The excitement almost all children feel when they are given the opportunity to do science provides the best starting point, but to keep that excitement alive the science that they do must continue to be seen by them to be relevant to them and of value in their lives.

5

Developing models for differentiated learning

Introduction

In earlier chapters I have argued that differentiation in primary science has been difficult since the introduction of the National Curriculum because it requires teachers to deal with two competing objectives simultaneously. The National Curriculum is subject-centred and hierarchical; it imposes a view of progression in each of the subject areas. Differentiation could be seen simply as sorting children in terms of the level of understanding they have reached along this simple vertical line of progression. However, teachers who need to consider the education of the whole child cannot approach differentiation in such simple terms. The teacher needs to take account of the individual in a variety of ways. Children may have the ability to work at a particular level in science but will need access to that work through the teacher reducing the reading and writing demands, or by a teacher providing a context that motivates children and allows them to access their own knowledge. A teacher may know that certain children or groups of children are mature enough to go on to work quite independently, which will enable them to progress further than other children, who may have the academic ability but not the social skills. All these factors influence the provision made for pupils by teachers.

When they are deciding the particular activities children will undertake, it is suggested that teachers start by finding out the ideas their children already have. These may not coincide with the predictions which the science order sets out. Thus a child might have an understanding of forces that matches some of that described at level 3 of the science curriculum, and may also express an understanding that suggests that he or she is nearer level 5. He or she may have an understanding that does not map on to the level descriptors or the programmes of study at all. The following idea might cause some difficulty.

Teacher: Why do you think the light bulb works?
Mandy: Because it comes out of the battery and goes down the wires to the light.
Teacher: What does?
Mandy: The stuff on the top of matches.
Teacher: Oh!
Mandy: Yes, and there's one of those strikers in the bulb.
Teacher: Is it like a candle?
Mandy: Yes, but it's posher.

This child has an understanding of electricity which allows her to explain why a light bulb comes on, and which would not hinder her in learning about the construction of different circuits, or the use of switches and other devices. This would then allow her to learn those aspects of the science order described in Attainment Target 4 for Key Stages 1 and 2 of the 1995 order. Should a teacher ignore this child's ideas about the tips of matches and simply go on to do circuits? The complexity of the task teachers face is what Ron Dearing was referring to when he said that 'Learning is a messy business' (Dearing 1993a).

In this chapter I want to try to draw together some of the issues discussed in the previous chapters. I will do this by first looking briefly at some of the more recent primary science schemes, and at the advice some other sources have to offer concerning differentiation. I will then examine the 1995 science order (DFE 1995) and consider how it might be used for planning that provides scope for differentiation. However, while it is easy to talk about differentiation, it is also important to see how it can be done in real 'messy' classrooms. The main part of this chapter will look at case studies where teachers have built differentiation into their teaching. In each case the teachers have tried to see differentiation not just as something which is done in one-off lessons, but as part of a programme of teaching. I will look at five different case studies in different ways. In the first I look at a single lesson with Year 1 children. The lesson was part of a topic on living things in a multicultural classroom. Here the focus was on providing access through shared experiences and language development. In the next I look at an example of one lesson in which a group of Year 2 children conduct an investigation. My observations focus on one quite able child and her behaviour during the lesson. The third case study also focuses on one child, but here the child is one who has some behavioural difficulties. In this case I have chosen to report on a series of lessons. These focused case studies are followed by two studies which trace some teaching through a full half-term, so that differentiation as something that is ongoing can be illustrated. One of these I have described in very great detail, the other in less detail, but with more examples of children's work.

Planning and differentiation

The introduction of the National Curriculum heralded the start of what might be considered the great hunt for a workable relationship between planning and assessment. Harlen *et al.* (1990) described the relationship between planning and assessment (Figure 5.1). I have modified the model a little to take account of changes in the science curriculum. This model, and variations of it, have been used extensively to describe how planning is informed by assessment. The view encapsulated in the model is presented in many primary science schemes. One very well constructed primary science scheme states that two of the purposes of assessment, among others, are:

- to monitor progress;
- to guide future provision of learning experiences.

One of the general principles adopted was that 'Assessment is an integral part of classroom activity. Some assessments will be

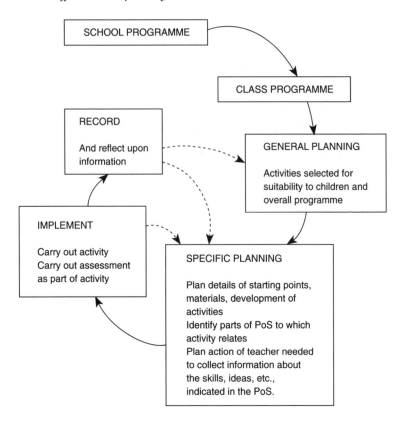

Figure 5.1   Model relating planning to assessment (modified from Harlen *et al.* 1990). PoS: programme of study

informal and not noticed by the pupils, others may be more formal and pupils' motivation may be affected by them' (Bath Science 5–16 1992). This scheme provides lots of ideas for science tasks and suggestions as to what aspects of the National Curriculum can be assessed in relation to each activity, but it does not indicate how the teacher should use that assessment. Another scheme (Oxford Primary Science 1993) provides suggestions for follow-up activities, but does not link these in any sense to the assessments made by teachers. If the model described by Harlen and her colleagues is to be taken seriously, then the teacher's judgements about individuals' progression as a result of some science experience would be used to determine the learning experiences offered to those individuals next. It would seem that the assessment support offered by these and other schemes is more for the purposes of monitoring and recording progress to meet the requirements of the national assessment system than to inform planning.

A popular scheme (Collins Primary Science 1990) implies that differentiation should be by outcome alone. In the teacher's guide for Key Stage 1 the possible outcomes for an activity to find out what materials sound will travel through are given as, for the more able child, 'Selects and tries out several materials – rejects some and considers others. Covers the clock, listens and adjusts to achieve satisfactory results.' The same activity for a less able child could lead to the outcome, 'Chooses materials randomly. Needs guidance to wrap clock. Shows no clear idea of effective and not effective materials.' The guide does indicate that the activities provided in the scheme are suitable for use in mixed-ability classes where some children have special needs. The activities are such that they can be adapted to suit children with short attention spans, as well as allowing for different outcomes, but they don't help the teacher in making these decisions. It seems to be that the published schemes, although recognizing the relationship between planning and assessment, cannot build in alternatives for the teacher. Teachers have to do it themselves.

One exception among the primary science schemes is the Nuffield scheme (Nuffield Primary Science 1993). This is based on the work of the SPACE project and the constructivist approach to teaching. In the teacher's guides for this scheme there are suggestions as to what a teacher might do as a result of the different ideas presented by children. They show the possible ways in which children's ideas could be followed up, using schematic representations. The Key Stage 1 teacher's guide on electricity and magnetism shows how, starting from the question 'Where does electricity come from?', children's ideas can lead to different activities. When a child or group responds to the question with 'It comes from the television' or 'It comes from the phone line', it is suggested that the teacher probes the children's understanding of switches and more generally of electrical appliances in the home. This might lead to a task being set for the children to find out about electrical appliances in the home and at school. Where children state that electricity comes from batteries, the children would be asked to think about things that use batteries and to make a collection of them. This approach encourages the teacher to use children's ideas as starting points, and suggests different routes. It does not go as far as to suggest how to group children, or how, depending on their initial ideas, they might take a different path through the content of a particular curriculum area. The problem is that, no matter what path a child, or group of children, takes through an area of the science curriculum, he or she needs, in the end, to have covered the content of the programme of study for that topic (unless he or she already understood it all). It is part of the teacher's role to work within what he or she understands the requirements to be, in terms of the content of the science order, to provide an appropriate path through. A scheme could never be this flexible. It seems, to use an anachronistic analogy, that a primary scheme has to be like a good girdle: it should provide sufficient support but leave plenty of freedom to manoeuvre.

The view that planning for the provision of differentiated experiences is the province of the class teacher and cannot be built into long- or medium-term planning is implied in School Curriculum and Assessment Authority (SCAA) publications. In the document *Planning the Curriculum at Key Stages 1 and 2* (SCAA 1995), the participants in a school's long-term curriculum planning are listed as the headteacher, governors and staff. Medium-term planning they see as the realm of the class teachers supported by subject coordinators, with short-term planning being carried out by the class teacher. The purposes of medium-term planning are to develop a detailed sequence of work for each year group, while the purposes of short term planning are to ensure:

- differentiation;
- a balance of different types of activity throughout the week;
- appropriate pace;
- time for teacher assessment;
- time for constructive feedback for pupils;
- monitoring, evaluation and (if required) modification of medium-term plan.

(SCAA: 1995: 10)

Inspection reports (OFSTED 1995) for the period just before the 1995 modification of the curriculum indicate that planning by teachers does not tend to show how they will provide for differentiation.

In the next section I present one suggestion as to how a teacher might plan to address one aspect of the revised science curriculum. I include in this some examples of children's work as it might relate to the planned topic. I do not, however, describe the topic in relation to the particular children involved, or in terms of the decisions the teacher made while the topic was being undertaken. I have done this to show how planning might be undertaken. But whenever a teacher plans, he or she plans with a particular group in mind. So I have included examples of the children's work to demonstrate what, as a teacher, I was anticipating when planning the work.

Planning for differentiation

The National Curriculum in science is now organized in key stages, with programmes of study (PoS) outlined for each key stage. Each part of a programme of study begins with 'Pupils should be taught . . .' This implies that the teacher must cover all the content of the PoS. Because the level descriptors are now so general there is clearly scope for a wide range of outcomes in relation to the PoS. Roy Richardson (1995) suggests that, when making assessments of children's performance using the 1995 order, teachers should 'not look for an exact fit to every single sentence within the level description, but instead find keys to making best fit assessments.' In the same way, the PoS are fairly limited in the clues they give as to exactly what should be covered. This gives teachers scope to plan work that is differentiated within the requirements for the key stage. The following section provides an outline of one attempt to plan for some work on green plants as organisms for a Key Stage 2 class. This meets the requirements of part of Attainment Target 2, Life Processes and Living Things.

In Key Stage 1 the PoS states that 'pupils should be taught that plants need light and water to grow'. As this was part of previous versions of the science curriculum, it might be assumed that the children in a Year 4 class have done some work on the factors affecting plant growth. Some will need to revisit this idea, and some will not need to, but will be ready to move ahead in their understanding. It therefore seems inappropriate to require all children in the class to undertake investigations to demonstrate that plants need light to grow. In Key Stage 2 the PoS states:

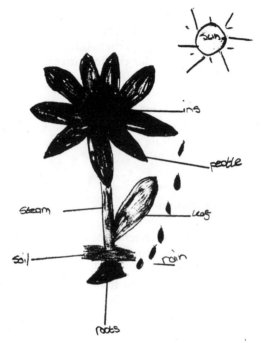

plants need light from the sun. plants give
us oxogine that we breath in we breath out charbon
diokide that we breath out this is called respartion

(a)

Figure 5.2   What plants need to grow: two children's drawings

Pupils should be taught that:

(a) plant growth is affected by the availability of light and
    water and by temperature;
(b) that plants need light to produce food for growth, and
    the importance of the leaf in this process;
(c) that the root anchors the plant, and that water and
    nutrients are taken in through the root and transported
    through the stem to other parts of the plant.

(DFE 1995: 9)

Initially it is important to find out what children's ideas are
at the start of the topic. A common approach to this is to ask the

(b)

class to draw a plant in a place where it would grow well and to label the drawing to show the conditions needed for growth. The Primary SPACE research (Russell and Watt 1990) showed that Key Stage 1 children mentioned only three conditions for growth (water, soil and sun), with few referring to all three. By Years 3 and 4 more children mentioned light rather than sun, and by Years 5 and 6 light was more common than sun. Very few children mentioned that plants need air, and most thought that soil provided support but did not consider that it also provided nutrients. This suggests that many children in Key Stage 2 will have a basic understanding of the requirements of plants, but could move on to more detailed exploration of their needs. Figure 5.2 shows some drawings made by children in a Year 4 class. Their understanding seems more advanced than that suggested by the

SPACE research data, which might have been expected, as these children started school after the introduction of the National Curriculum, and have had a very good science education. These children had completed the Key Stage 1 programme of study and were at the time nearly half way through Key Stage 2.

The drawings made by children in this Year 4 class indicate that most had an understanding of what plants need to grow. Using the evidence of children's ideas a teacher would be in a position to encourage different groups of children to move towards different activities around the same general theme.

Figure 5.3 shows a plan which begins with the teacher asking the general question, 'What do plants need to grow?' The variety of different responses to this question, either represented in the children's drawings or uncovered during group or whole-class discussion, might be those indicated in the oval boxes. Further questioning and discussion might lead to more questions being raised by the children, and then on to investigable questions which do not all start from the same point. Thus the teacher might group together children who understand that plants need soil, water and light to grow. Some may suggest that soil is simply there to support the plant. They might go on to try growing a plant in water alone. The group would need to think carefully about how they would go about this investigation: holding up the plants carefully, comparing them with plants grown in soil, ensuring that all other relevant factors are controlled. They would also need to find a way to record their evidence over a period of time. Figure 5.4 shows a planning board developed by one group of children exploring the function of leaves in food production. Many schools and local authorities now use devices of this nature to help children to plan their investigations. They are based on a suggestion by Wynne Harlen (1985), which she took from the Science 5–13 project 'Working with wood' (1972).

Each group would work on a different investigation. Those considering their idea that plants need the sun's light to make food might be encouraged to grow radishes. These grow over a period of three to six weeks. The children could grow radish plants in dull, semi-shaded and very light conditions and then weigh the resultant radishes to see which plants have been able to store the most food. Another group might grow two lots of radishes, but keep removing some of the leaves from one group over the growing period, or cover some leaves with foil. The resulting

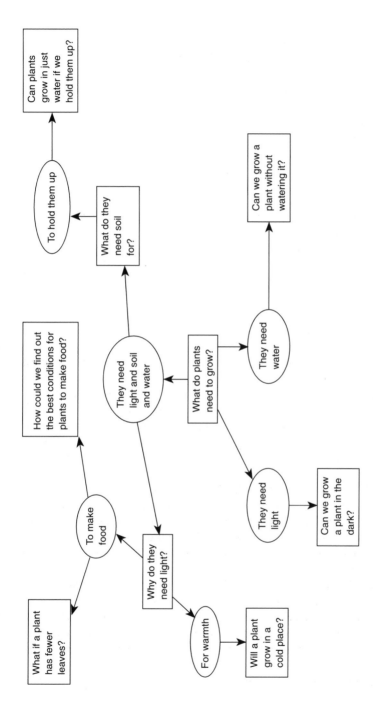

Figure 5.3 Plan for differentiated work on plant growth

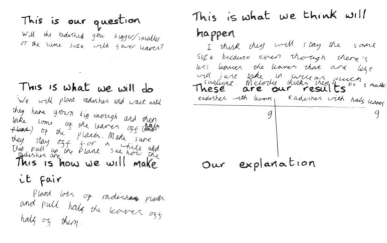

This is our question

Will the radishes grow bigger/smaller or the same size with fewer leaves?

This is what we will do

We will plant radishes and wait until they have grown big enough and then take some of the leaves off (half) of the plants. Make sure they stay off for a while add then pull up the plant see how the radishes are.

This is how we will make it fair

Plant lots of radishes plants and pull half the leaves off half of them.

This is what we think will happen

I think they will stay the same size because even though there's less leaves the leaves that are left will just take in twice as much sunlight. Melody thinks they'll be smaller.

These are our results

radishes with leaves | radishes with half leaves

9 | 9

Our explanation

Figure 5.4 Planning board: do plants need leaves to make food?

radishes could be weighed and compared. Other children would simply attempt to find out the effects of lack of light or of water. The groups might write up their findings in the form of a class gardening magazine to help others to get the most from their plants.

During the course of the work on plants children will have an opportunity to develop their ability to plan, carry out and record findings for an investigation based on their own ideas. The teacher would have the opportunity to observe the children as they plan and carry out their investigations. He or she might, in discussion with a small group, be able to judge whether a child was able to turn her or his own ideas into a form which could be investigated, or turn ideas suggested to her or him into an investigation. In the case of the radishes it is unlikely that children would think to use this plant and to weigh the radishes as a means of judging the effects of different conditions. However, the children could develop their skills in collecting and using evidence, and would be able to decide on the apparatus to use.

During the course of the topic the teacher would also have the opportunity to assess the children's developing understanding of growth and nutrition in green plants. Regular discussions about how groups are getting on, in which the whole class might sometimes participate, would allow the teacher to ask questions about the conditions for growth. It would also enable children to find out what others in the class are doing and to learn from them. A final presentation of a group's work could take the form of a page in a magazine for the young gardener prepared by the children. A teacher who has not been able to collect verbal evidence from every child in the class might decide to return to the initial activity and to ask each child to draw a plant and describe the ideal conditions for growth. This would allow an assessment based on what the children have learned, not only from their own investigations but also from those of others.

The above discussion represents one person's thinking when planning to teach one aspect of a topic. It is not messy enough. The following case studies were undertaken over a period of three years on visits by me to different teachers' classes. The interpretation of the lessons observed was only possible because teachers gave me a great deal of their time and were willing to spend time talking to me, and sharing with me their thinking before, during and after lessons.

CASE STUDY 1: Differentiation with an emphasis on language

Living things: a single lesson focusing on teaching science in a multicultural school

The class

The class of 5 to 6 year olds was in an inner-city school in a very deprived area. The children in the class were from several different cultural backgrounds. The class was small, with only 18 pupils. However, one child had Down's syndrome, and a further four already had statements of special educational need drawn up for them. The school has a policy of working very closely with parents and there is a parents' centre to which each class goes a couple of times a week to undertake lessons supported by parents. The school is also involved in a scheme to provide education for parents, with systems which can lead to accreditation through the Open College.

The topic

The school has a policy of taking children out of school as much as possible to provide them with a wide range of experiences (this is funded through the LEA). For the younger classes this generally means a visit once a week. During the year teachers had arranged trips to supermarkets, to art galleries, to the park and many other places. The topic for the half of the term was living things. During that topic the children had visited a local park, and been taken to a larger park in the city and shown around by two rangers. They had also spent an afternoon in the natural history museum. The topic was to culminate with a weekend trip to the LEA's field centre in North Wales. On the day when the lesson reported here took place, the children were very excited about the weekend away.

The classroom showed the evidence of the work the children had done on living things. Bean plants were growing furiously from a bag of potting compost. Zig-zag books containing pictures drawn by the children of the bean plants as they grew, with measurements, were pinned on the wall. Mathematics, counting ladybird's spots, and observational drawings and plasticine models of small animals were everywhere (see Figure 5.5). There was also a vivarium containing snails, and another for caterpillars.

The teacher started the morning off with a fairly long discussion about living things.

Teacher: I was out very early this morning on a hunt for minibeasts. I hardly found any because . . .
Sunil: It's too hot.
Teacher: They like it, how?
Farouk: Cold.
Teacher: Not cold like winter, but cool. I have got some snails.
Nikita: They have got holes? [The child had not had chance to look at the snails yet.]
Mark: For air.
Teacher: Yes.
Sara: They need air.

The class went on to discuss the snails they already had. They planned to clean out the container, to get them some fresh food and then to release the ones they had had for some time and replace them with new ones. The discussion continued as the

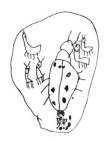

Ranjit
The lava eat
greenfly.

(a)

Snails
mate

as They
cling together
eurh snall
shoots
white dart a small
into the dart
Shaills both

(b)

Figure 5.5 Work by Year 1 child on minibeasts

teacher took out one of the new snails. They talked about the number of rings on the snail and how this told them its age. It had five rings, so they concluded that it was a similar age to the children in the class.

Teacher: Oh, look what it's done on me!
Massak: It's done a poo.
Teacher: It doesn't matter, does it? Everything has got to poo.

The teacher then read the children a book from a scheme the school had just purchased. It showed different animals and plants that might be found in a garden. The child with Down's syndrome arrived in class and was asked to tell the class what he could see. The lesson continued.

Yasmin: Caterpillar.
Sunil: Ladybirds.
Teacher: Good.
Farouk: A worm.
Teacher: Come and point. Where is the worm?
Farouk: In the soil, they like the dark.
Teacher: Earthworms like the damp earth. What does damp mean, Karina?
Karina: Bit wet.
Teacher: Yes, not very wet, just a bit wet.

The class then went on to discuss spiders and how they wrap up their prey and then make 'a sort of fly soup out of them', which they drink.

The discussion demonstrated that the children had a firm grasp on many of the processes of life. The children understood the notion of a life cycle, knew that living things grow, reproduce, need food and excrete waste. However, most noticeable in the discussion was the way in which the class teacher checked the children's understanding of different words. She did not assume that they all understood 'damp', and she made sure that 'cool' was understood. This arose quite naturally in the discussion. The care taken by the teacher to ensure that children knew the meaning of everyday words was also employed in dealing with words associated with the topic.

Teacher: Manjit, is a snail an insect?
Manjit: Hasn't got six legs.
Teacher: Carly, is a tadpole an insect?

Carly: No.

Teacher: What does it grow into?

. . .

Teacher: Ayat, is a bee an insect?

Ayat: It's got three parts to its body.

Mark: Abdomen.

Teacher: Yes, one of the parts is its abdomen. Well done.

. . .

Teacher: Can anyone think of any more insects?

Rob: A snake.

Teacher: Not a snake but a . . .

Rob: . . .

Teacher: Begins with a 'w'.

Rob: Worm.

Teacher: Is a worm an insect?

Here the teacher explored the children's understanding of the characteristics of insects. She had given the children the more scientific words to described the body parts, but did not expect them all to use them. Mark, one of the most able in the class, was able to pick up and use such words, while Rob was still struggling with the word for worm. In another class a teacher might have brushed aside the suggestion that a snake is an insect, but the class teacher recognized the confusion here between worm and snake and attempted to clear that up before exploring whether a worm is in fact an insect.

After the discussion the teacher introduced the work the children would be doing after they had been out on a brief minibeast hunt. One group was to work on a language task. Another group was to draw and stick pictures of living things on a collage. The collage was to be lent to another teacher to use with her class. Another would paint pictures of minibeasts to send to the park rangers as a thank you. One group, of children who had not yet done so, was to make sketches of the new batch of snails. The teacher said later that the children produce better work when they can see a purpose or use for the product. The groups were selected with regard to a number of factors: who would work well with whom, which activities would motivate particular children, how many could work on a particular activity at a time. They were not necessarily selected to reflect ability groupings.

The class teacher explained how she organized the groups.

I don't have fixed groups, and I don't always move them all
on to another activity together. Today I could sit with the children doing the language work and the others could get on
pretty well. That meant I could let each one finish and then
decide where to move them on to. I could call up one or two
children when I thought it was right, and talk them through
the work. Sometimes I have to move them all on at once, but
the range of abilities in the class makes that difficult.

The class teacher knew where everyone was, although half of the
class were out in the shared working area. The classroom assistant, shared between three classes, was available to help out. One
child, described as very able but needing support with English,
painted a large black spider. He showed it proudly to the teacher.
She admired it, and counted the legs out loud. There were eight
of them. She then said, 'Is that its head?' This prompted the boy
to comment that he had forgotten the abdomen. The teacher asked
him where he would put the abdomen, and he knew and went
away to add it. Another child looked at her painting and noticed
that she had forgotten to put legs on her butterfly, but then only
added two. One child spent the whole of that part of the lesson
with the snails. She continued to be fascinated by them, discussing them with other children as they arrived. The teacher explained that this child had a very deprived home life. In that she
had so few experiences, she needed a long time to explore things
and to delight in tactile and visual experiences. The child also
had a very short attention span for written work and needed a
lot of support from the teacher to do any writing and reading.
The teacher set aside time to work with her later.

The main features of the work of the class teacher included a
detailed knowledge of all the children, their home lives, their linguistic abilities, their specific and general learning difficulties and
their specific abilities. In all her work with the children she was
clearly listening to them carefully and interpreting their responses
in the light of what she knew about each individual. It was also
important to provide some shared experiences on which the children could build, rather than to assume that all the children had
been to a park, or had spent time discussing the living things
around them. It was clear throughout the lesson that the teacher
kept in mind the science concepts she wanted the children to
develop. It was not simply a language lesson dressed up in a

science context. The children had developed an understanding of the concepts of the processes of life. They could discuss these processes confidently, and could apply them to different animals and plants. In this lesson differentiation was not pre-planned, in the sense that different children would be given very different tasks; rather the teacher modified the tasks for the children through her individual or small group input. The teacher explained that this was not always the case: sometimes she provided different worksheets or completely different activities.

CASE STUDY 2: Differentiation by outcome

Cars down ramps: a single lesson focusing on one child

The setting for the next case study is a very large primary school in a working-class area. The summer term topic for a class of 31 year 2 children (7 year olds) was road safety. The subject focus for the topic was geography rather than science. However, within this topic there was some work on forces, looking at cars travelling on different surfaces and on slopes. The class teacher used a mixture of teaching styles. Some of her teaching was whole class, such as story time or learning about the Green Cross Code. Some of her teaching was with mixed-ability groups, such as in poetry writing, 'where children can spark ideas off each other'. Sometimes she used ability groups, such as when she taught phonics. At other times she would give differentiated work sheets, allowing the children to choose their own working groups. The lesson I describe here was an integrated one with some children working on maths, some illustrating the Green Cross Code and others making a final draft of a poem.

One group of children was extracted to do some science work. The eight children were considered by the teacher to be the more able in science. She explained that she had tended to use mixed-ability grouping in science earlier on in the year, when the children were working at levels 1 and 2 of the science National Curriculum for Attainment Target 1. But as some children began to develop an understanding of fair testing and became able to make predictions, she began to group them together to work on investigations.

After lunch the teacher talked to the whole class, reminding them of the work they should do in the afternoon. The teacher then quickly settled the rest down and came back to the science group. She explained that science is very demanding of teacher time, so it could only be done when the work given to other children made fewer demands on her time.

Introduction

The teacher began the discussion by putting a toy car on the floor.

Teacher: How can I make it move?
Rupert: Push it.
Nigel: Pull it.
Teacher: Any other ways?
Paul: You could give it a shove.
Teacher: Is that the same or different than 'push?'
Paul: No, it's a push.
Teacher: Any other ways?
Lizzy: You could go down a slope.
   . . .
Rupert: Was that what you were thinking?
Teacher: Yes, that's what we are going to do. What would happen if I put it on a ramp or a slope?
Lizzy: Where's the slope?
Teacher: What could we do? Any ideas?

None of the children spoke – they were thinking.

Teacher: What does a slope look like? [To Ryan.]
Ryan: Hill.
Lizzy: We could use multi-link blocks.

The teacher then explained that she had borrowed some big blocks from another class and had a big sheet of perspex to run the car down. She did not get these out at this point but carried on the discussion.

Teacher: Why do we need blocks?
Rupert: To hold it up.
Teacher: How far will it go?
Ryan: To the bottom.
Teacher: Can we make it go further?
Holly: You could make it steeper.
Teacher: Try to make it not very steep, and then steeper. What do you think?

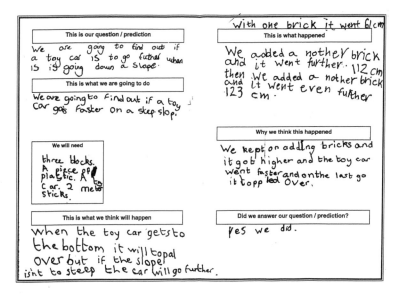

Figure 5.6 Planning board: comparing slopes

Paul: It will go faster, because if it's steeper, how fast it will go normal if you make it steeper it will go faster.

The children and teacher carried on discussing the investigation for a time, thinking about what the question was they were going to ask, and what prediction they wanted to make. The teacher then took out a planning board, which is designed for children who are working broadly at level 3 of science Attainment Target 1 (see Figure 5.6). They discussed the headings on one side of the page; the other side would be completed after the children had finished their investigation. In all this time, Lizzy, who had offered so much at the start of the discussion, said nothing. She fiddled with her fingers and her dress, and did not seem to be listening.

Group work

The children then went back to a table to work together on completing the planning board. The teacher assigned a different child to write each of the four sections. They were to discuss their answers, then write them down. There was much discussion, and it did seem that all but two of the children were contributing. Lizzy went to the toilet, then when she came back she sat seemingly dreaming. Martin did not say anything, but seemed to be listening most of the time, and he nodded when he agreed with a statement. But as soon as the writing was completed Lizzy took the toy car and went to sit where she thought the top of the slope would be.

The teacher rejoined the group and asked another child to try the first run. Lizzy did not get a turn for some time. At one point the car hit a child's foot at the end of its run. Lee began to measure the distance from the base of the slope, but others realized that another run was needed. Lizzy went to take the car, but Rupert said that it should be Martin's turn again, so he could do it the same. Lizzy accepted this logic. Most of the interesting action was at the other end of the slope where distances were being measured. So she moved over to that side. She did not push her way in, but stood back trying to see. On one occasion the children could not decide if the reading was 165 cm or 166 cm. Lizzy suggested, 'You could put, and a half, 'cos that's in between.' The teacher picked this up and asked how a half is written. Some children responded. The teacher checked Paul's understanding, and he wrote $165\frac{1}{2}$.

Lizzy saw her chance to take a turn: 'Mrs Green, can I have a go next time?' The slope became higher and on Lizzy's first try the car toppled over. Ryan was delighted, but Nigel suggested, and the other children agreed, that Lizzy should try again.

Before play time the teacher encouraged the children to think about what had happened, so that they could begin to write up the investigation after play. Lizzy tried out a response: 'It went faster and further with three blocks.' After play the children were allocated scribing jobs, so that they all had a turn. The first heading was 'This is what happened'. Leanne was writing. Lizzy began:

Lizzy: As we added a brick on.
Ryan: No, we added another brick.
Lizzy: No, listen to me. As we added a brick on, it went further.

Leanne wrote, 'We added another brick.'

Leanne: What do I put after brick?
Ryan: Then we added another brick and it toppled over.
Teacher: If we added another brick, what did we do before that?

Paul: It went just far with one brick.
Teacher: So, with one brick it went? And then we added.

Leanne added a line above the first. The discussion continued with Lizzy taking full part, but allowing Ryan and Nigel to override her suggestions. Finally it was her turn to write an answer to 'Why we think it happened', and she graciously agreed to include the information Ryan so badly wanted to include.

This group of children collaborated extremely well, although the teacher felt she still needed to allocate turns for writing. Lizzy, it seems, likes to take the lead; if she is not leading, she tends to cut herself off. But, unlike Ryan and Nigel, she does not tend to dominate. The teacher explained that they have a tendency to dominate the group, and write down what they want to write. On a number of occasions during the lesson the teacher commented on this: 'Are these boys being bossy again? Are they, Holly?' The teacher explained that she had tried single-sex groups, but this had not helped because 'it's not always gender at this age. Martin, for example, is very able, but he's also shy. He understands very well, but does not contribute to discussions. In groups of "bossy" boys he has less opportunity to speak out.'

Lizzy, like the other three girls in the group, did not push her way forward at all, but looked for opportunities to make her mark. It would be interesting to see how she gets on as she gets older. The tendency to retreat is already there.

The group members were encouraged to work together. It seems that here the teacher was not providing differentiated experiences, but purposely attempting to give the children the same activity and to allow the outcome to be the same. However, during the activity the teacher did manipulate the situation. She asked Paul, the least able in the group, to keep the record. She encouraged Leanne, who had a clear understanding of measurement, to measure with Holly, who found it more difficult. She tried to make sure the children shared the work, and that Nigel, who worried about spelling, should have Rupert's help.

In addition, the teacher keeps a small notebook in which she records some of the things the children say during an activity. Once the work is completed she takes photocopies of the planning board, giving one to each child. She then writes notes on the back of each sheet of paper. On this occasion she wrote

Ryan: Very sure the car would topple over. Agreed that one try was not a fair test.

Leanne: Made very careful measurements, making sure the end of the ruler was at the bottom of the slope.

Lizzy: Predicted that the steeper the slope the further the car would go. Interpreted the results. Understands the idea of a half.

These assessments are kept in the children's files, but recorded by the teacher against National Curriculum science criteria, to indicate the general level at which each is operating. Thus, within this group it might be said that differentiation was more by outcome. However, other groups would be given a simpler version of the planning board, depending on the previous assessments made of the children's performance.

CASE STUDY 3: Differentiation with an emphasis on the individual

Electricity: a series of lessons focusing on one child

A teacher makes many decisions about how lessons will be conducted. Some of these are taken at the stage of medium-term planning, others as a result of how one lesson went, others during the lesson, either in response to the way groups of children work or in response to the needs of an individual. In this section I will concentrate on one child, during a series of lessons on electricity.

A teacher who was new to a class of year 5 children was taking them for a series of six lessons on electricity. The school was in a deprived inner-city area. The class was unfortunate in having a high proportion of children with difficulties of various kinds. In consequence the science the children had studied had been formal, with much writing and little practical work. The first of the six lessons was one hour long and the rest were of two hours' duration. The teacher's initial plan, which is a little more detailed than the medium-term plan described by SCAA (1995), was, in brief:

Lesson 1   Setting the rules and explaining expectations. Introduction to the idea of electricity – general discussion.

	Introducing the idea of a concept map. Each child to make a concept map for electricity.
Lesson 2	Whole-class discussion around the questions: What does electricity do? What is electricity?
	Introduction to the basic equipment, the symbols for electricity and the correct use of equipment.
	Working in small groups, general play with equipment. Children asked to find a way to make the bulb light, then to draw a picture or a diagram of the circuit and attempt to write an explanation of what is happening.
Lesson 3	Circus of activities relating to circuits (looking at conductors, insulators and resistors).
	Class discussion to share observations and ideas.
Lesson 4	Investigating switches and trying to use these observations to think about what a circuit is (what is happening).
	Whole-class presentation of the idea of circuit diagrams, to ensure that they can all do them, rather than pictures. Constructing own circuit diagrams, attempting to use the diagrams drawn by others to build a circuit.
Lesson 5	Continuing with work on making different circuits (parallel and series), looking at brightness of bulb etc.
	Discussion about how mains electricity works, then shift to focus on safety.
Lesson 6	Assessment tasks to be carried out individually.

The teacher's own fuller plans for the six lessons included links with the programmes of study for science, and made mention of resource requirements and classroom organization issues.

The child I will concentrate on is a 10 year old boy called Charles. He was an immature child who produced little or no written work, although he did not have reading or writing difficulties. Whenever he lost interest in the lesson, or felt that the demands made on him could not be met, he quietly took out some paper and continued with a drawing of a boat or plane which he always had in his drawer. Often when the teacher was introducing the lesson he took out his drawing, was spotted and asked to replace it. He then took it out a few minutes later. The class teacher described this as a coping strategy Charles had developed in order to keep himself out of mischief, and to help him keep calm when in previous years he might have behaved badly. He sat at the back of the class on a table with two girls who talked to each other incessantly, when they were allowed. He did not mix with the other children in the class and when he did speak to the girls it was often to throw insults.

Although the general plan was adhered to there were many changes in response to the children's progress. No differentiation is indicated within the general plans, but the teacher grouped and regrouped children throughout the series of lessons in accordance with her assessment of their performance.

The first short lesson had four purposes: to introduce the teacher, to set the rules for working practices, to give the children confidence and to get them to think about their own ideas about electricity. The teacher set the scene by explaining that she wanted to see the class working together in groups, developing their understanding of electricity by talking about what they were doing with each other and thinking all the time about why things happen. The teacher explained that, for her sake, she would need to have written evidence of their thinking so that she could make decisions about what to teach next, or about who could move on and who needed extra help. This approach was entirely novel to the children. The teacher asked the class what they knew about electricity. The children were taught how to make a concept map. They then thought up some words they associated with electricity, then each developed his or her map. This was very difficult for many children. The teacher explained that they were to put down what they think: 'If that's what you think now then put that down. Later as we go through you may think to yourself "I was right about that" or you may think "I need to think that over again".'

At the beginning of the lesson the teacher asked Charles if he was OK sitting at the back, and whether he would like to move. He did not answer but shifted on his seat to indicate that he would stay. Later, a boy sitting near the front told the teacher about a book he had taken from the library about electricity. He had previously shown it to the teacher. He had difficulty describing an interesting point made in the book, but the teacher helped him along. She then said to the whole class:

It is difficult sometimes to say what you mean, to find the words, but I have been teaching a long time and I can often help. I am interested in your ideas, so it doesn't matter if you find it difficult to say it, I can help. I want to know what your ideas are.

During the introductory discussion the teacher directed the odd simple question at Charles. These questions almost invariably required one word answers. She gave him a great deal of encouragement and praised him when he answered. When the class began their concept maps, she moved across the room and said, 'Are you OK, Charles? Do you know what to do?' He nodded and the teacher then asked the other children on the table if they were OK too.

The second lesson was intended simply to allow the children to explore the equipment associated with electric circuits, to make a buzzer work, a motor spin and a bulb light. The children were asked to work in pairs. The teacher decided who would work with whom. The children were put into single-sex pairs. This was to ensure that girls were not excluded by boys, who tend to take over the equipment. The teacher made the decisions about who would work together because the children were not very good at making such decisions. One girl was a loner and often excluded, yet when paired with a more confident girl who helped her manipulate the equipment she worked well and gained a great deal of satisfaction from lighting a bulb. Charles was allowed to work on his own. The teacher explained that he found it very difficult to work with others and that he needed to build up his confidence. This lesson was ideal, as there were few demands on him to write anything down. With much encouragement he did make a most concerted attempt, towards the end of the lesson, to draw a diagram of his circuit (see Figure 5.7).

During the third lesson the teacher gave out workbooks for the children to use. These consisted of a series of worksheets linked to a circus of activities set up around the classroom. The intention was to encourage independence, with the children making decisions for themselves about which activity to move on to next, deciding when they had completed one activity etc. All the activities required the children to think about what happens and why. For example, one activity consisted of one cell (battery) and two bulbs connected in series. The activity sheet was set out as in Figure 5.8.

Charles wrote very little on any of his activity sheets. He did

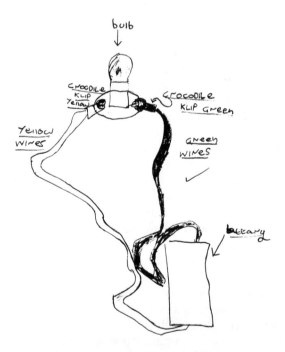

Figure 5.7   Charles's circuit picture

Activity 3

What do you notice about the brightness of the bulbs?

Are they shining as brightly as when there was one bulb in the circuit?

Why do you think this happens?

Draw a circuit diagram to show the circuit.

Figure 5.8   One activity in a workbook provided for the children

try to work round a number of the activities, but tended to retreat to his own table, where, with some spare batteries and a
bulb, he made a couple of different circuits.

The teacher gathered in the workbooks at the end of the lesson for marking. At the start of the fourth lesson the teacher
explained to the class what she was going to do and why.

> We spent some really good time last week because people
> were talking, people were thinking, people were doing. But
> what I got from you in terms of work written down didn't
> show that. This week we are going to work in a different way.
> I have decided on three main groups. I made that decision
> based on the work you gave in, what you did last week and
> what you need to know to move on.

The teacher identified one group as those who had not engaged
with the request to put forward their ideas about how a circuit
works, and so had not tried to explain why the bulb lights. This
group also included children who had not made drawings of the
circuits they had made on their worksheets. The second group
included children who had made attempts to understand how
circuits might work, but had come unstuck because their ideas

were causing them confusion. These children were to work in pairs on selected activities from the workbooks. The activities selected involved simple circuits in series, including switches etc. They were to work on certain tasks from the circus, undertaking one activity at a time, writing it up and then going to the teacher to discuss it before moving on to the next. The final group included children who had progressed well in the previous week. The teacher explained to them: 'I want you each to work on your own. From what you did last week I can tell you have got a good level of understanding. Then I will call you back to me so we can discuss your explanations.' She felt that this would help to build up their confidence in themselves as learners.

The teacher set the class working, gathering together the six children who needed to look again at the simple circuit. The group was gathered together around one table. The teacher sat down with them. She had one of the worksheets. She asked Charles to go across the room to get her a battery, some wires and crocodile clips, and a bulb.

Emma: Miss, he will forget.
Teacher: Why?
Emma: He always forgets.
Teacher: Perhaps he needs practice.
Emma: Oh?
Teacher: I am teaching him to remember.

Charles was collecting equipment from the box and looked over to the teacher, who slowly reminded him of the list of things, saying 'You know all the things we need to make a circuit.' When Charles returned she made little comment, saying, 'Good, we can make a start.'

The teacher asked the children if they knew how to draw symbols for a bulb, battery and wires. She did not ask Charles at this point. She then asked one girl to make the bulb work.

Teacher: What has she done to make the bulb light?
Pupil: Connected.
Teacher: How?
Pupil: She put the two crocodile clips to the screws on the bulbs.
Teacher: Yes, but what are we doing?
Pupil: There is power from the battery through the wire and to the bulb.

Teacher: Now what have I done? [Disconnected the wire to the battery.]
Pupil: Taken the power from the battery.
Teacher: Is there still power in the battery now?
Charles: Energy.
Teacher: Yes, Charles. Will the battery run out of energy now? [Charles did not answer, but shook his head almost imperceptibly.]
Pupil: The battery will run out if the light's on.

The teacher encouraged the children to think about what was going on and to come to an understanding that a complete circuit was needed. She then asked them all to draw a circuit using the appropriate symbols. She told the children to go back to their seats and to write down the conclusion to their discussion. They were asked to write, 'To make the bulb light there has to be a complete circuit.'

By the time the first group had moved off children from the second group had finished their first activity and wanted to discuss it. The teacher then circulated the first group, finding that three of the children had forgotten what it was they were to write. The teacher then rehearsed the ideas with them, because she felt that they would have been able to remember this simple sentence had they fully grasped the concept. Charles had returned to his place and had begun to write his sentence. He wrote 'To make a bulb'. He then asked for the spelling of battery and was given it on some scrap paper. He then got out his incomplete drawing of a car and started to colour it in. When the teacher arrived he put it away. She asked him what he was going to put next. He said battery. 'What will you say about the battery?' He replied, 'You need battery and wires.' The teacher praised him and asked him to write that down. He was clearly encouraged by this and wrote his sentence. This was something of a breakthrough.

Once the teacher was satisfied that all the children in the first group could draw a circuit and had grasped the idea that a complete circuit was needed, she asked them to go back to working in pairs, attempting, and writing up, one activity at a time. Charles began well. He collected batteries and bulbs and returned to his place to work on one of the activities. He did not seem to be confident enough to move around the tables working. Unfortunately, he became involved in an argument with the girls on his table. This put him off and he reverted to playing with the batteries and taking no notice of the activity sheet.

The fifth lesson began with some general discussion about the activities carried out during the previous weeks. The teacher revised with the children the idea that a circuit needs to be complete for a current to flow. She talked about switches and what their effect was, then extended the discussion to include the light switches in mains electricity. A number of the children had not made the connection between switches breaking the circuit and what might be happening in the light switch in the classroom. Charles did not behave well during this lesson: he returned to his drawing several times. He could not cope with the whole-class discussion. However, at the start of the second part of the lesson, after break, the teacher asked the class if anyone could explain what was needed for a complete circuit. Charles raised his hand and said, 'It has to be connected. The battery has to connect to the bulb and the bulb back to the battery.' The teacher could hardly contain her excitement. This was the longest speech Charles had made, and it was made in complete coherent sentences. Charles was very pleased with himself and did not take out his drawing until later in the lesson, when the teacher had to deal with another child who was giving cheek.

The series of lessons described here did not result in a great deal of written work from Charles, or from some other members of the class. Another child, a girl, who was often disheartened by her own lack of progress, was able to explore some of her own ideas, with the support and encouragement of the teacher. Certain children in the class were given the opportunity to progress at quite a rapid rate: they were able to describe how some materials conduct electricity well, others do not conduct it well and others are insulators; they had begun to understand the difference between circuits connected in series and those in parallel; and they were able to speculate about the nature of electricity. The series of lessons was not a complete success as far as all members of the class were concerned. In evaluating the lessons at the end, the teacher came to some conclusions about the kinds of strategies she might use on other occasions with particular children. It is clear that without the concern for the individual exhibited by the teacher, and the recognition of individual needs, these movements forward would not have been possible.

CASE STUDY 4: Differentiation using children's own ideas for investigations

Differentiation: a topic on toys

The class

The school is situated in a deprived inner-city area. The class consisted of 25 children (7 year olds), all but one having English as their home language. A number of children in the class have special educational needs, although at the time none had actually been given a statement of special need.

Sue runs an integrated day, with science activities taking place on three days of the week. The children were in four groups, sitting according to their reading attainment on entry to the class. Sue was clear that this did not correspond to ability groups. In discussion she pointed out the children she had found to be progressing well in science.

> Leon and Malcolm (group 1) are really doing well, they could tell you five variables to control no problem. Phanni and Sally (group 2) are very good, they can question and predict. Gerard is mathematical and accurate (group 3). Peter is coming up and Hilda is terribly sensible. Georgie is quiet but she knows what's going on (all group 4).

The children tended to work with others in their groups, because only one group did science at a time. However, when the teacher had more than one group working on science, she did mix them, or let them mix themselves.

The topic

The topic for the whole term was toys. This was a cross-curricular topic, involving maths, English, technology, history, music and PE. The science plans for the whole term included work on toy cars, bouncing balls, rolling balls, magnets, toy boats and electricity. Sue's plans for a topic include ideas for differentiation. Figure 5.9 shows part of her science planning for the first part of the toys topic.

At the start of the topic Sue discussed toys with the class. She encouraged them to think about the way different toys move.

YEAR TWO PLAN – TOPIC TOYS

What the children will learn	Activity	Evidence
Children will have experience of devices which move,	*Toy cars* Initial play activities involving ways of moving the variety of vehicles provided – to ascertain children's ideas of push, pull. Put on a slope etc.	Children able to say if push or pull is needed in variety of vehicles. Can they mention 'gravity'?
	Much opportunity for discovering which car travels furthest down a slope.	Ability to test idea: draw a conclusion, say it/write it.
and manufactured forces such as those produced by wind up toys, elastic or electrically driven toys.	Which surface on the slope is best? Does the steepness of the slope affect the distance travelled?	Can follow on from general toy sorting. Can child find those which have own energy source and those which need a push or pull? Able to communicate this verbally.
	Find ways of getting the cars to travel on a flat surface (group children according to ideas). Find ways of getting the cars to travel *up* the slopes – elastic power etc. Again, group similar ideas together.	
These forces should be experienced in the way they push, pull, make things move, stop things and change the shape of objects.	**Differentiation** This occurs naturally from discussion. Split into ideas to test *or* ways of measuring e.g. using cms, independent measuring, or several measures to give a total, according to ability. Opportunities for fair testing.	

What the children will learn	Activity	Evidence
	Maybe own ideas or mine according to ability.	
	Further work may be attempted and may be suggested in discussion by *more able* children. Investigate ways of stopping the car, e.g. how many blocks are needed etc.	Able to think of an idea to test. Able to tell the teacher that a force is needed (push/ pull) to stop or slow the car.
Level 3 – they should experience the natural force of gravity pulling things down.	How thick? How far is a stationary car knocked by a moving one? Investigate adding weights to cars moving up and down flat surfaces.	
That a force is a push or a pull, that gravity is a force which pulls things down.	*Bouncing Balls* Collect a wide variety of balls. Discuss, sort, group and explain. Ask children to think of some ideas about the ball which they would like to test.	Child thinks of one idea to test.
Develop skills in fair testing, measurement, and observation.	Split the groups into subgroups according to their ideas/level of complexity. The children may suggest following. 1. Bounce some balls on different surfaces. Does surface affect (a) Number of bounces, (b) height of	
Develop ability to explain observations	bounce, (c) how long the ball bounces for?	Child able to make observations and record.

What the children will learn	Activity	Evidence
	Differentiation Measuring more complex for some. Fair testing by some. Own idea or mine.	
	2. Investigate the height of the drop of the ball on same surface. Then on different surfaces.	Child can explain that a force is acting on the balls.
Understand that a force can change the shape of things	3. Investigate dropping of different balls on same surface (also sand) which ball is best? Children may wish to count the bounces, or the level of the highest bounce. 4. Try using balls of plasticine (change of shape).	When using plasticine balls, child can explain that a force can change the shape of object.
Develop skills in measuring time. Develop fair testing. Further understanding of friction	*Rolling balls* 1. Investigate rolling balls down slopes. Change the height of the slope – measure time of arrival of ball at rest. 2. Try changing the surface of the slope versus time, or change the ball rolled.	Child thinks of a change in variable.

Figure 5.9 Sue's plans for toys topic

The children brought in some examples of moving toys. Sue added to these. A display was started of toys that move. The classroom in which Sue works consists of one half of a very large old school hall. The other half is still used as an assembly hall. Sue makes good use of this space, for display and for sending toys travelling long distances. The children were then given lots of opportunity to play with the toys, to try them out. They were encouraged to think about what makes the toy move.

The children worked in groups, and after they had had some initial play time, Sue used the opportunity to make an initial assessment. She was looking to see which children could say that a push or a pull was needed to make the toy move. She was also looking to see if anyone mentioned gravity. At this point she was able to identify two groups of children within the class: those who could use the words push and pull appropriately, and those who needed some extra support to develop the appropriate language. 'Some, you could see, understood the concept, because when I asked them what was needed they showed me a push or a pull, but they used the wrong word. They needed more experience with the words. More discussion and trying out.' Sue then worked intensively with the children who were unsure. She felt that they would not be able to raise investigable questions unless the concept of a force as a push or a pull was in place.

Those children who had a good grasp of push and pull were able to move on more rapidly to working with other toys. They sorted toys and considered where some toys got their energy from. In order to move the children on to investigations, Sue worked with groups, discussing their observations about the toy cars. She encouraged them to think about how they could compare the different toy cars they had. This led to a investigation in which a whole group was involved. In pairs the children measured how far their chosen car would go down a slope. Sue encouraged the children to add up the total distances of each run of a car for comparison. This is quite a difficult task, so stretching the abilities of those children who were more able in mathematics. Figure 5.10 shows the resulting chart for one group. This activity was not particularly differentiated. However, it did help to develop in the children some of the skills they would need to carry out other tests of their own. Richards (1995) suggests that one should provide children with lots of experiences before moving towards an investigation. Thus, he suggests, at the beginning of a topic on materials children should be allowed to play with dough, water and such like. Sue uses a similar approach, but setting the amount of time and the amount of teacher intervention according to the needs of groups of children.

Sue uses two main strategies when moving towards investigations. She often discusses children's ideas with them as a group,

Type of car	1st go cms	2nd go cms	3rd go cms	Total cms
	110	60	160	330
	45	55	60	160
	25	75	95	195
	100	40	70	210
	35	40	30	105
	51	60	82	193
	22	25	35	82
	40	70	85	195

Figure 5.10 Group record of distance travelled by cars

writing down the different questions they raise. Then, usually in pairs, the children go off to test out their ideas. Sometimes the children discuss their ideas one day and then undertake the investigation on the next day or later that day. This gives Sue time to draw up a number of different sheets related to different children. Sometimes the worksheets are the same for different groups, but are open-ended enough to allow for different degrees of sophistication in the investigation. An example of the latter was the investigations resulting from the question: 'How far can we make a car move along on a flat surface?' The children thought about how they were going to make their cars go. Some suggested blowing, flicking or setting them off with an elastic band. Sue had a sheet prepared for the children to complete. One pair of children suggested that they could blow the cars and see how far they went. With some encouragement they decided to compare two cars, blowing both (Figure 5.11). This investigation made few demands on the children to make measurements. They could have compared distances travelled directly. However, by encouraging a comparison, Sue had given them the opportunity to consider the need for a fair test.

Another pair of children was able to suggest making a comparison between different ways of making the car move. They suggested flicking, blowing and pushing (Figure 5.12). The same worksheet was used for both groups of children, but the investigations were appropriate to their level of understanding.

An alternative strategy employed by Sue later in the topic was to develop different worksheets for children according to the questions they raised. For example, children were encouraged to think about how they could make a car move up a slope. Some children were able to think of different ways in which they could do this, and decided that they would like to compare the different ways. Others were only able to deal with comparing two ways of making a car travel up the slope. Some were not at a point where they could explore the differences systematically. The first group were given a worksheet on which they could list three different ways to move the car (see Figure 5.13). Another group only had two ways to deal with. Others, who were less able to deal with an investigation, were asked to try out different ways, and to report to the teacher. Some wanted to record their observations in paint (see Figure 5.14).

As the topic progressed, Sue offered children the opportunity

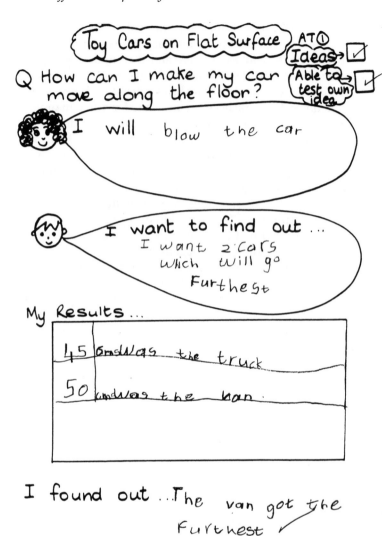

Figure 5.11 One child's worksheet showing different ways of moving a car on a flat surface

Figure 5.12 One child's worksheet comparing one car with another when blown

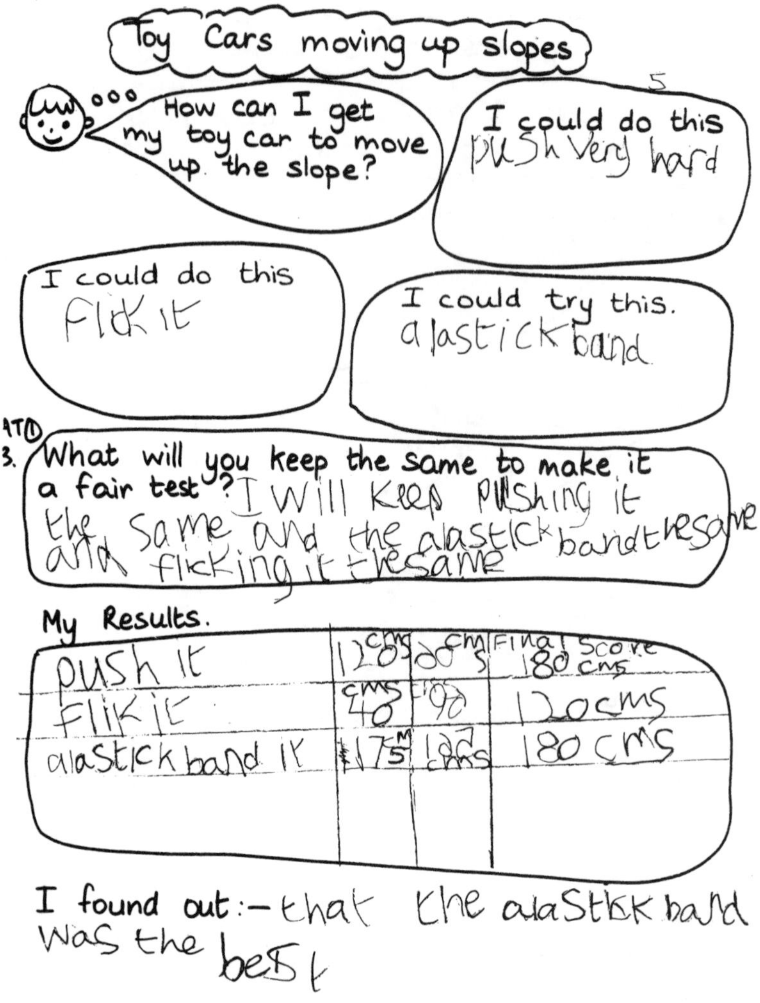

Figure 5.13 One child's worksheet looking at different ways to get a car to move up a slope

to extend their understanding of forces and of the processes of investigation through an exploration of balls bouncing. The activities that the children were encouraged to undertake included finding out which of several balls bounces highest, which surface is the best for bouncing balls on, the effect of different surfaces

Figure 5.14 A child's painting of moving a car up a slope

on how balls roll, rolling balls down tracks (curtain track beaten into different shapes) to explore the effects. Again differentiation was brought about by encouraging the children to raise their own questions where possible, and helping them to identify an investigation they could carry out and achieve satisfactory results from. Thus some children, when testing which surface a ball bounces best on, counted the number of times a ball bounced. Other children were able to bring their skills in measurement to bear by measuring the height of rebound of the ball from each surface.

One of the crucial factors in Sue being able to differentiate in a way which is flexible is through her ongoing assessment. On her plans for the term she notes the main outcomes she is looking for. For example, one activity looks at the number of journeys a ping pong ball and a ball bearing make when set off on a 'U' shaped curtain track. In her plans Sue lists the kinds of questions she will ask of the children: 'Does it matter where the ball is released?' 'Try different balls at different heights'. In the 'evidence' column of her plans she indicates that she would be looking to see if a child 'thinks of a question and tests it – level three' or 'can test a question given – level two', She has a hardbacked notebook in which she writes the children's names, arranged in the working groups operating at the time. Along the top of the page she lists the criteria she is particularly interested in. During the lesson she listens out for particular comments, or looks for evidence in the ideas the children put down on paper. Then she takes a few minutes during breaks to tick off who has met the criteria. This running record is used in her planning. She uses it to work out who needs some additional help, and who could work with whom in order to push them on further. This record is then used at the end of the year to complete the summative assessments, which are then passed on to the next teacher.

The work done by Sue's class was extensive and varied. The time taken with those children who were not firm in their understanding of pushes and pulls paid off, as it enabled all the children to move towards their own investigations. Unless the initial concepts are firm children are not in a position to raise their own questions. The children showed a pride in their work and had developed a questioning attitude. They were eager to try things out, because they felt capable of doing so and knew that this was valued by the teacher. The pupils' sense of ownership of the investigations they were undertaking was further fostered by the inclusion of much science reporting at 'sharing assemblies', which the infant classes have regularly. This ownership was achieved by the teacher ensuring that the tasks undertaken were appropriate to the individuals and that the ideas were theirs. This seems to be a crucial factor for achieving lively learning in primary science.

CASE STUDY 5: Differentiation by continuous teacher readjustment

Materials: a half of one term topic

The next case study is a report of one teacher's attempt to research an approach to providing for differentiation (Webb and Qualter 1996). She considered it important to see differentiation in ongoing terms, with children moving forward in different ways throughout the half term. This meant that she needed to use assessments made of children immediately to modify a lesson as it progressed, and to help her plan the next lesson's work. In the following report I have focused on two aspects: classroom organization and the kinds of decisions made by the teacher as she directed children in different ways.

The class

There were 22 children in the class, ranging between the ages of 9 and 11 years (Years 5 and 6). They were of a wide range of abilities, from children who were considered by Gail to be within the broad band of having special educational needs, including one child with a statement of educational need because of learning difficulties and another for whom a statement of need was being sought, to a couple who were extremely able. Three children were visually impaired; one, an able 10 year old, was classified as blind for educational purposes. Another, a boy, had some vision, but had other associated learning difficulties. The third child was considered to be of average ability but behind because of his visual impairment. Support was available for most science lessons from a specialist teacher from the visual impairment (VI) unit.

The topic

The school scheme required the teacher to cover materials, focusing on the idea of natural and manufactured materials, and on the notions of permanent and temporary change. Gail also planned to focus on developing the children's skills in planning and recording evidence, two aspects of investigations which she felt the children needed further work on. The topic was spread over a four week period, it being a short half term. There were three hours of science per week; that is, one whole afternoon and an hour on another day. The general plan for progression through the topic is shown in Figure 5.15.

The class teacher wanted to see how far she could go in providing differentiated experiences for the children. She decided that she could not do this at the level of the general medium-term plan, but needed to modify her plans as she went along in response to the children. During each lesson she made notes about the children's performance, and took their work home to look at; then she planned her approach to the following lesson. These plans were written down and included lists detailing the groups individuals would work in, notes on the timing of different

Knowledge	Skills
(a) Natural and man-made. Materials at home and at school (PoS AT 3iii).	Observation Recording
(b) Exploring change of state. Making jelly: children were asked to plan how to change jelly from solid to liquid to solid again. Carry out investigations, observe and record observations. Discussion about change of state.	Planning Use of equipment Observation
(c) Change of state: investigating melting chocolate.	Recording
(d) Permanent change: investigating the action of heat on eggs.	Fair testing
(e) Change of state, temporary. Investigation of different types of sugars and how they dissolve.	Measuring Raising questions Predicting
(f) Assessment: using investigation on soap powders and chocolate.	Recording
(g) Research work on how things are made. Extension activity: investigation into chemical change using plaster of Paris.	Explaining All skills above Constructing fair test Planning/investigating Hypothesis Explanation

Figure 5.15 Gail's general plan for progression through the topic

activities and details of which group she would work with and when. There were also notes such as 'Put the kettle on, make sure children know it's on and don't go near it.' I thought at the time that this was done because I was coming to watch the lessons, but in fact this teacher regularly plans in this much detail when trying out a slightly new approach.

It is nearly impossible to report on a series of lessons in as much detail as is needed to get a real feel for how the teacher and pupils interacted. In the following subsection I have tried to give some indication of how the topic went in the first two weeks. I then go into quite a lot of detail about one lesson. This was the lesson in which distinct groupings began to separate out. Prior to that only two different levels of tasks were being set. In the case of lesson 3 the same basic task was set to all pupils, with some differentiation built in to the materials provided and much ongoing differentation provided by Gail.

Lesson 1

1 Aims: to introduce the children to the idea of classifying materials as natural and manufactured; to introduce the idea of states of matter; to develop skills of planning, observation and recording.
2 Grouping.
   - Group 1 (seven children), least able children, including one child with visual impairment.
   - Groups 2 (eight children) and 3 (seven children), of a similar spread of ability but each forming good social groups.
3 Activities.
   - The lesson began with a whole class discussion of materials and their origins. This moved on to a brief consideration of solids, liquids and gases. The children then worked in groups.
   - Group 1: listing objects from school and home and noting the materials from which they are made.
   - Group 2: using words on cards to build up a chart of naturally occurring materials and manufactured materials, with the raw materials from which they were made. Followed by work on the jelly investigation.
   - Group 3: undertaking the jelly investigation. They were asked to plan how they were going to observe the jelly, before

and after hot water was added, and how they were going to record their observations. This was followed by carrying out the investigation and then by a word sorting exercise.

Gail began by working with group 1, helping them to start discussing the materials different objects were made of. She then moved over to work with group 3, who had spent some time thinking about their investigation, and how they were going to record their observation. Once group 3 was on its way, group 2 was visited and Gail discussed this group's chart. The children then wrote up the chart while the teacher moved back to group 1.

The children in group 1 generally worked well on the sorting task, but one girl (considered as having special educational needs), found it very difficult to stay on task. Some children had not used jelly before and took longer than expected to do the task, so the prediction of when there would be high levels of demand by different groups was a little off.

Lesson 2

1 Aims: The children would be taught that some things change temporarily, and some things change permanently. They would revise the idea of manufactured and natural materials. The processes focused on included raising questions, observation and drawing conclusions.
2 Grouping.
   - Group 1: five children who had had difficulty making and recording observations during the previous week's activities.
   - Group 2: three children who were visually impaired (so that they could share specialized equipment, as difficulties had arisen in the previous lesson in catering for their special needs).
   - Group 3: seven children who had produced work which showed that they could bring their previous knowledge to bear on their sorting and classifying, and were able to use science skills appropriately.
   - Group 4: seven children like those in group 3, but tending to include more of the older children in the class.
3 Activities.
   - Sorting manufactured and natural.
   - Observing eggs cook (permanent change).

- Observing chocolate melt (temporary change of state).
- Developing an investigation related to chocolate's change (raising questions and planning).

Group 1 was given a card sorting activity, while group 2 was given a worksheet asking questions about natural and manufactured materials (enlarged and designed with the help of the VI teacher). Gail then worked with groups 3 and 4 to explain the worksheet and to do the observation of eggs activity. Gail then moved to groups 1 and 2 to work with them as they did the heating chocolate activity. While these two groups recorded their findings the work done by groups 3 and 4 was looked at and discussed, and the heating chocolate activity was set up. Then Gail worked with groups 1 and 2 as they did the chocolate activity. The extension activity for some in groups 3 and 4 was given to children who successfully completed the other activities (mostly group 4). The children were asked to raise questions, for an investigation, about the melting of chocolate. This is an activity children in this class were used to, as raising questions is identified as one of the skills of science within the LEA.

The three visually impaired children were of very different levels of ability. The problem of sharing resources was solved, but the group did not cohere socially or in terms of ability, so they tended to demand much more teacher attention than they would otherwise have done, and did not progress as well as expected. Gail was worried that they were relying too much on the VI teacher and not developing the ability to work independently.

Some of the children in group 1 found it very difficult to get beyond observation to speculation. Gail was concerned that,

> If they can't get beyond straight observation then I can't see how they will be able to progress in the knowledge aspects. I might have to devise a whole different set of activities for them, which will make them look different from the other groups, which I don't want to do.

Groups 3 and 4 were all able to deal with complex instructions and some went on to plan investigations.

Lesson 3 in detail

The focus of the lesson was the development of process skills using the phenomenon of sugar dissolving in water as an example of a temporary change. Gail places great emphasis on process skill science. She commented at the beginning of the lesson that the way she teaches process science

> is a far cry from the way process science was originally envisaged. I now use a very structured approach. I identify the particular skills I want to develop and I give structured worksheets and teaching input so that the children are in a position to do the required investigation.

In this lesson she wanted to focus particularly on the skill of recording findings. She had decided to provide some of the children with a recording device to complete, but with others would attempt to discuss the problem and encourage them to develop their own records. If any children seem to be floundering, Gail said, 'that is the point when I have to go in and teach them how to record or whatever'.

Grouping

Three groups were arranged for the purpose of classroom organization. Group 1 (seven children) consisted of most of the children from the original group 1, but group 2 included five children who worked well together and who had shown themselves to need more structured support with planning and recording work. Group 3 therefore included ten children who generally worked in four separate groups.

Introduction

The children arrived back from morning assembly to find saucers containing five different kinds of sugar arranged on the tables. The children were clearly expecting this and sat down quickly ready to start. The children sat in three areas of the classroom so that the groups could come together easily for discussion.

Group 1, the least able group, was given a worksheet on which to record observations. The class were told that they needed to look very carefully at each of the sugars, to find out all they could from observing them, as this was crucial to the investigation. Group one was told to begin observing the sugars straight away, but not to draw them until Gail had time to demonstrate how to use the hand lenses.

Groups 2 and 3 were drawn together. They were given a sheet listing the tasks they would be undertaking during the session. Gail asked one child to read out the first task. She asked if there were any problems. She emphasized that one of the purposes of the activity was to make detailed records. She also checked on the children's understanding of the word 'dissolve'. She asked children to read the different tasks out in turn and checked understanding of terms. She commended the group on the good standard of work done in the previous week. She then turned to the whole class to discuss the names of the various sugars being studied and to get ideas from the children about why castor sugar, for example, is used in making cake icing.

Gail then went over to sit with some children in group 1. She showed them how to use the hand lens and discussed what they were observing. One child had already made a drawing of a circular saucer with a mound of sugar on it. Gail then suggested he rub this out and start now to focus on the individual bits of sugar. She spent some time with one girl. A statement of special educational need was being sought for her and she used this opportunity to assess the child's understanding of this task and her ability to follow very simple instructions in using a hand lens.

Gail then moved away from the class, saying that she needed to see that they were all on task and knew what they were doing. They all needed to spend time observing and discussing their observations. One child from group 3 asked why they needed to draw the sugar so close up. She explained that it is what the sugar is like close up that is important when thinking about how it will dissolve.

Using observations to make predictions (groups 2 and 3)

As it became clear that the class was moving towards completion of the sugar observation, the teacher drew groups 2 and 3 together. She discussed their observations with them.

Teacher: Laura talked about different shapes.
Simon: Some are piles, some are scrunched up.
Vicky: It comes from sugar cane.
. . .
Mandy: Small fragments, really small.
Jamie: The icing sugar is small and fluffy.

David: Feels different.

Gerard: Some bigger, some smaller, some big crystals, some small.

Vicky: They are all crystals, but some are more ground.

Gail then went on to ask which of these factors might affect how well the sugars dissolve. She asked the children to think about this problem individually and to write it down. She then added that if they felt able they could also 'put in a because'; that is, why they think a particular factor might be important. The children worked on in silence, as Gail moved to do the same activity with group 1. She returned to the group with, 'Now, it's amazing how much we can learn from others.'

She then revised the previous discussion, identifying the factors which the children had brought out. She asked the children in turn to report on their thinking.

Alex: I think bigger and harder sugar will take longer to dissolve because I think bigger and harder sugars will take longer.

Jamie: I think icing sugar will dissolve because it's fluffy and fine, because it's made to dissolve.

Simon: I think the difference that affects how they will dissolve is how small they are . . . because small will spread.

Vicky: Cube takes longer than granulated because the grains are squashed. The demerara will take a long time because the grains are bigger. The bigger the grains the longer.

The bell for play time rang at that point. The children found the idea hard to drop. A number held back to discuss their ideas with the teacher; others were heard talking about it in the playground; a couple came in early with some thoughts. After play time Gail set them the task of planning an investigation to test out their ideas. She emphasized that they would need to decide how they would find out which dissolves best, and they would need to decide what they meant by *best*.

Using observations to make predictions (group 1)

Again, with group 1, Gail asked the children to describe their observations.

Ian: The caster sugar sprinkles

Gail said that she knew exactly what he meant, and then went on to rephrase his idea to explain that the grains are very fine and so spread out around the central pile of sugar.

The children in this group focused initially on icing sugar: 'it is lumpier than the rest', 'bigger than the rest', 'softer than brown sugar'. They did not identify granule size as a factor. Gail decided to leave the group for a while so that they could reconsider the differences between the sugars. When she returned to them to continue the discussion, two children in the group who worked together began to put forward the idea that the size of the granules of sugar might make a difference. However, others in the group did not move away from discussion of the sweetness of the sugars, or the feel of the sugars. They also talked about when they had eaten the sugars etc. The teacher moved them on to talk about how they might find out which dissolves best. She asked them how they would decide what *best* meant.

Mick: Which would go in a cup of hot tea.
Cleo: Which would go fastest.

The children in this group did not come up with any ideas as to what might constitute best. Consequently they were given a very structured worksheet to follow. The two boys who had begun to explore the idea that the granule size might make a difference were taken through the worksheet separately and asked to make predictions on the basis of granule size. The worksheet included instructions to get beakers with equal amounts of water in them and to add a spoon full of sugar and time how long it took for each to disappear. They were given a recording device to use. The two children in the group who were able to discuss the possible effects of granule size on dissolving were not able to turn their question into an investigable form. They were given the same worksheet as the others, but asked to work together. Gail said of the rest of the group: 'They are just doing pure observation. There was nothing I could get hold of to get them into questioning and investigation.'

Planning an investigation

Gail gave groups 2 and 3 the opportunity to plan their investigation, but, as the children in group 2 began to firm up their ideas, she joined them. She focused on the record sheet the children would need to use. She had come to the conclusion, from previous lessons, that they would have difficulty devising their own. She discussed the structure of such a table with the children, but realized that they found this task difficult. At this point she took out a model record sheet to show the children. They were given one each so that they could stick them in their science books. 'I would have liked group 2 to do their own record sheet, but they found it too difficult. Mandy is very lacking in self-confidence although she is quite able,' Gail said.

She hoped group 3 children would be able to devise their own record sheet. All the children in groups 2 and 3 were given an outline planning sheet on which they wrote down the question they set themselves, the equipment they would need, how they would make the test fair, what they would observe and what they would measure, their prediction, with reasons, and how they would record their observations. Planning took some time to complete and the children worked very hard thinking about what they would do.

After having set the children the problem of planning their investigations, Gail did not call the full group together for discussions but circulated among the working groups discussing their ideas with them. One girl raised the problem of the cube sugar. She was concerned that the cube would 'go' in two stages, first it would need to break up to expose all the granules of sugar to the water. She felt that once this had been completed it would dissolve at the same rate as ordinary granulated sugar. Another boy from group 1 had discussed the same idea with the teacher during play time. Gail called him over and asked if he would like to work with Laura on this problem. He was keen to do so. She asked them to work on a separate table, slightly removed from the others. She later said:

> I thought those two were mature enough to get on with a complicated investigation like that. Vicky might have been up to it too, but with her vision problems she couldn't have coped. I didn't want them to work with the others because I think they would have been confused with the idea of two variables.

The other children in group 1 were encouraged to devise a table in which they could record their results. Gail felt that they should be able to manage this after the amount of time she had spent on the subject. Two girls, Vicky and her partner, needed a little support to reassure them that their table was fine, and to remind them that they needed to think about how often they would make an observation. Two boys sitting together, Darren and Alex, went along quite happily and were able to draw up a table with little difficulty. Gail said later: 'I felt I didn't pull Darren and Alex in. They are both very bright, but reticent about giving ideas out. I don't think they picked up as much as the others. They didn't take their thinking as far as the others. They sat a long way away, I should have moved them closer.' Two boys struggled with the drawing up of a table. Gail spent time with them helping them to think through what they were trying to find out. One of the two made a start, but could not complete it; the other could not even begin. Finally Gail drew their charts for them. Later she commented on the 'vast difficulty' of drawing up recording devices.

As the session progressed the differences in the actual tasks the children were carrying out grew. By the end of the session group 3 included: two children carrying out an investigation involving two independent variables; eight children looking at the same experiment, but with two having trouble working out how to time their observations, four having some trouble developing a recording device and two needing them drawn for them. Group 2 worked as a group, but needed a lot of teacher support to figure out what to measure and how to record it. Group 1 simply followed instructions, although two members of the group were able to make a prediction about what would happen on the basis of grain size.

Lesson 4

This short lesson involved all the children in observing the effects of adding water to different powders, and the kinds of changes taking place. The children also considered the question 'Could we get it back?' This was a teacher-directed activity rather than one devised by the children. The intention was to show permanent and temporary change, where water was added to plaster of Paris and to talcum powder, for example.

Lessons 5 and 6

These lessons involved the same groupings of children as emerged from lesson 3. The focus was on developing process skills. Gail wanted to use the lessons to assess the children on their ability to plan and carry out an investigation. The least able children were asked to plan an experiment to find out what happens to chocolate as it melts. This involved a review of something they had already observed. The other groups were asked to find out about different soap powders and how they dissolved. Gail explained to the children in groups 2 and 3 that they were on their own, because she wanted to observe them to make an assessment. In this way, Gail was able to assess the children on their process skills.

During lesson 5 and the following short lesson 6 Gail extended her assessment of the children's understanding. She sat with small groups of children in turn as they observed the mixing of vinegar with baking powder, and vinegar with soap powder. She chose this particular activity because it would allow her to assess their observation skills and to judge how far they were able to speculate about chemical change. As is common practice in the class, Gail told the children that she was using the session as an opportunity to assess their progress. She made notes throughout, interrupting the discussion only to clarify a point. The children were clearly used to this.

Gerard: Rises and goes back.
Della: Acid is like polluted water, it has strong things, like smell, that makes things happen.
Darren: Vinegar irritated the chemicals in the baking powder and the soap powder, vinegar is an acid. Soap powder might have something in it that stops the acid working and so it just dissolves the powder.
Lee: Vinegar is more of a chemical than water, vinegar has got acid in. Acid disintegrates fragments of baking powder.

Lesson 7

At the beginning of the following lesson the teacher commented, 'It's become more differentiated now because last week some of them were coming up with the idea of chemical change. I am not sure if they will get the idea fully but I am letting them do it on their own to see how far they go.'

Some of the children from group 3 seemed to grasp the idea

of chemical change. These children were encouraged to plan an investigation to test out their ideas that some sort of permanent change had occurred and that something different had been made when vinegar and baking powder were mixed. Further work with children in groups 2 and 3 included looking at a candle burn and considering why it went out when under a jar. This led to discussions about combustion. Again some children began to see that a change could have occurred which was permanent. Some children who had not really grasped the idea when just presented with the vinegar and baking powder began to come to some understanding. They were asked to plan an investigation to find out if something is lost or something gained when things are burned. They could not carry this out because the equipment was not available. Some of the children in groups 2 and 3 did not grasp the idea of chemical change. The teacher gave them work to consolidate their understanding of change of state and of manufactured and natural materials using secondary sources.

Gail felt that the five least able children had gone as far as she could take them. She said, 'If they can't get far with the basic process skills there is no way they can develop the knowledge of things like temporary and permanent change, and they couldn't possibly get to understand chemical change.'

The last lesson in this series was, for this group, merely a handwriting and copying exercise. This worried Gail. She felt that this group of children needed to move on to another aspect of science after the third session, rather than trying to move further in their understanding of materials.

Conclusion

This series of lessons, in which a teacher tried to build in a flexible approach that would ensure the provision of appropriately differentiated learning experiences, proved to be extremely complex. We realized that good social grouping and the development of the ability to work independently were crucial to the progress of individuals. Thus, although it is inappropriate to ignore the difficulties experienced by children with a handicap (thus Gail decided that Vicky would find it too difficult to do the investigation with the cube sugar, although she might have been able enough), arranging for them to have appropriate aids is effective, while grouping them together irrespective of other characteristics is not effective. The teacher needs to have a clear idea of where he or she wants to take the children in terms of both process and concepts, and needs to be aware of the different strategies to employ to achieve these. Duggan and Gott (1994) argue that different types of practical work serve different purposes. Observation work (such as the observation of the sugars and the observation of vinegar and baking soda mixing) promotes the development of conceptual understanding, as does practical work designed to illustrate a point (such as the exercises in mixing water with different white powders). Investigations promote both conceptual and procedural understanding. It is also clear that the level of motivation of the children, and their engagement with the topic, is important (Alex and Darren were able enough to develop further than they did, but were happy to coast along). The classroom environment is important in providing a situation in which the children feel comfortable enough to express their ideas and to make suggestions as to what they might do. Some children who lack confidence, even in such classrooms, do not progress as far as they otherwise might (Mandy, for example, should have done better but lacked self-confidence).

Emerging models for differentiation

The case studies discussed above are not examples of perfect teaching. They are examples of teachers struggling to achieve a workable approach to differentiation. I selected the particular case studies because they provided different clues as to how differentiation might be achieved. In different ways and to differing extents they incorporate some of the issues that were raised and discussed in previous chapters. No doubt different readers will highlight different things from the case studies, but the points that strike me are:

- All the teachers had a clear idea of the science concepts they wanted to teach and had developed a route that they wished to follow to ensure progression. For example, in the minibeasts topic the teacher emphasized the processes of life, underlining them in discussion.
- None of the teachers had rigid plans; all were able to keep a clear view of the science they were teaching while being able

to respond to individuals needs. For example, in the toys topic the teacher had very detailed plans, which included phrases such as 'differentiation – this occurs naturally from discussion'.

- The processes of science were central to the teaching. For example, in the materials topic the teacher did not believe that the children who could not raise questions about materials which could be investigated could develop their understanding of permanent and temporary change much further.
- All the teachers kept notes as they went along on their assessments of the children's understanding. For example, in the cars down slopes lesson the teacher made notes throughout and transferred them on to the child's individual copy of the afternoon's work.
- There was a strong emphasis on collaboration. Teachers took time and were at pains to ensure that children worked together and learned from one another. In some case studies and in other examples in previous chapters teachers were clearly making this a top priority. In the electricity topic the teacher struggled to set up an atmosphere where children felt confident enough to share ideas. In this case it meant building up individuals' confidence and slowly working towards a more collaborative atmosphere.
- Teachers relied on shared experiences as starting points. Sometimes these were provided through initial play activities, sometimes simply through discussion and in one case by the school providing these experiences for the children as part of their topic. For example, in one inner-city school the children were taken out regularly to provide these shared experiences. In the materials topic, the teacher took time to discuss children's experiences of different sugars, to encourage them to bring that understanding to bear on their thinking.
- There was a good deal of evidence of teachers focusing on language development. This was done in two ways: first, by modifying worksheets or other materials to provide access for children, and by ensuring that the children understood basic concepts; second, using discussion and exploration to establish the meaning of words and to link this meaning to science concepts. In the toys topic the teacher took time to ensure that the words 'push' and 'pull' were firmly established and understood.
- There was a strong emphasis on the teacher understanding the

individual, in terms both of their understanding of the science concepts and of all the other factors that might influence their learning. Thus a child was allowed to sit for a long period exploring snails. Another child was given practice in remembering a list of things to collect so that the teacher could set up a circuit.

This list is by no means exhaustive. In the final chapter I will take this discussion a little further to present a model to describe the processes of differentiation.

6

The process of differentiation

Introduction

It is striking that when we talk about differentiation we tend to mean either providing for children of different abilities or providing equality of opportunity. Yet the two are inextricably linked. Teachers need to understand their pupils. The observation of lots of teachers teaching science has brought this home to me more than anything else. It seems a shame that practising teachers do not get the opportunity to observe others teaching. Watching others teach and, most importantly, discussing that teaching, sharing ideas and thinking together about one's own teaching and that of others is surely what it means to be a truly reflective practitioner. The introduction of the National Curriculum has helped in one way. It provided a common, if nearly impossible, agenda for teachers to plan together. This shared planning is valued by many teachers because of the sharing of ideas and experiences. The trouble with dealing with the issue of differentiation is that many teachers say that they do not know how to do it in science.

Yet when I sit and observe teachers, they are all differentiating to some extent. Building on what we already do, rather than using simplistic models for differentiation, is more likely to lead to individual teachers developing an approach that is sustainable. Differentiation is not something that is simply done at the initial planning stage. That is part of it, but it is a process that continues throughout the teaching of any content to a particular group of children. It is apparent at all stages of teaching. A teacher needs to ask different questions at each stage in that process. Below I outline the various stages in planning and teaching a topic and the questions the teacher needs to ask herself or himself.

Planning a topic

What material will we cover?

The first level of planning is the key stage or the school. Together a group of teachers will decide what aspects of the curriculum they want to cover with different classes of children. The starting point for planning the particular aspects that one year group will cover will depend on the coverage that the children have achieved earlier. The assessments that a teacher makes, which are passed on to the next, should provide a useful picture of the general level of understanding of the children in the class. One point that has emerged from looking at teachers planning in recent months is that it cannot be assumed that children in Key Stage 2 are starting with no previous school experience of a topic. So a year 6 class will need to take a topic such as electricity further than wiring up a bulb in a circuit. They are likely to have done this in Key Stage 1, and revisited it earlier in Key Stage 2.

How will I make it relevant to all the children?

In selecting a particular topic the teacher needs to consider the content and choose the way the content will be presented. Thus, the question that needs to be asked is what the children in the class find interesting and relevant. If the content is forces, then for younger children the topic might be toys. For older children a topic that focuses on road safety might be more motivating. Just addressing forces without some overarching theme is likely to appeal to fewer children. Girls will be more motivated and will be able to access their prior knowledge more readily if they see the relevance of forces to road safety. The discussions in Chapter 4 suggest that boys would also be more interested in road safety than simply forces. When working on any topic the teacher needs to consider how, as part of that topic, the interests of all the children in the class can be tapped. Discussions about food, for instance, should include foods eaten by all children in the class and by people from cultures not necessarily represented in the teaching group. In this way children's interest in the wider society in which they live can be satisfied, and avenues opened for them.

What is the progression in the science topic?

It is most important when he or she is planning the topic for the teacher to have a clear idea of the progression in the science that is going to be covered. A clear understanding requires research. The National Curriculum provides a starting point, but it is essential that teachers undertake research on the topics they intend to teach. This is where planning as a team can be so helpful. Some primary science schemes include a section on background science. Other useful materials are available to help the teachers to develop a deeper understanding of the background science (e.g. Schilling *et al.* 1991).

What prior experiences are the children likely to bring, and what will they need for this topic?

The teacher will need to decide on the extent to which children in the class will be able to bring prior experience to bear on their work. Would all members of a class of children doing a topic on sound be able to start with investigations of string telephones? Or would they need to spend time exploring sound makers and developing their understanding that sound has a source and that it travels? Will the children have prior experience of making jelly? The materials topic outlined in Chapter 5 demonstrates that flexibility is needed on this because we are not always correct in the assumptions we make. Can a topic on living things start with an assumption that a class of children know about the variety of life that there is in the school grounds, or in a park?

At the end of this stage the teacher, or group of teachers planning together, will have a general plan of the topic. This plan needs to be clear, but flexible. It also needs to fit into the time available.

Exploring initial ideas

What do individuals in the class already know?

A group of children may have studied a particular aspect of the curriculum before, but their understanding will not necessarily be the same after a gap as it was at the end of the previous topic. The children will have continued to build on their ideas both outside and inside school. Some will need to revisit earlier work; others will be ready to move on. For the teacher, finding out children's ideas is essential. However, it needs to be carefully done so that the information can be used to help weekly planning. In Chapter 3 I outlined some different approaches that teachers could take when finding out children's ideas. I also discussed how teachers can make use of these ideas. Again it is necessary for the analysis of the responses made by the children to be linked to what it is the teacher wants the children to learn. Otherwise, the vast array of different ideas can be daunting. Thus, for example, how children represent sound is less important than whether they represent sound as travelling, and as having a source.

How will I find this out?

It is not always necessary to ask children to carry out a specific assessment activity to find out their ideas. Much can be achieved through discussion. However, it is important that discussion with groups or with the whole class does not 'average out' the different ways in which the children in the group understand a concept. This can mean that some children are not able to keep up with the group, while others are held back. In the example of work with plant growth given in Chapter 5, the initial ideas of the children were used to provide stimulating investigations for children starting at different levels.

One of the outcomes of the project to evaluate the implementation of science in the National Curriculum, with which I was involved (Russell *et al.* 1994), was that teachers found it difficult to design the kind of formative and diagnostic assessment activities that I discussed in Chapter 3. There are many examples of activities that can be used to find out children's ideas. These have often been used by people undertaking research, rather than by teachers in classrooms. The activities designed for research purposes can be adapted by teachers for their own use. It does mean that we need to experiment with different approaches and different strategies for interpreting the evidence. This will take any teacher and school time to develop. The SPACE research reports (e.g. Osborne *et al.* 1993; Russell *et al.* 1993) could be useful here. The work of the Children's Learning in Science Project (CLIS 1984–91), which focused on older pupils, is also a valuable source of ideas. I have used many references to *Primary Science Review* in the preceding chapters, because there are many suggestions for approaches to teaching based on children's initial ideas reported in the journal.

Grouping

What approach to grouping shall I adopt?

How a teacher groups a class is determined by a wide range of factors. From discussons on this issue with teachers it is clear that very rigid grouping (for example, based on reading ability) can make it difficult to group children for other subjects. Teachers often comment that children can have good ideas in science despite having difficulties with reading and writing. The correlation between ability in one aspect of the curriculum and another is not high. However, a balance needs to be achieved. Thus, in a small class of Year 1 children in a multicultural school there were no fixed groupings at all. Children worked in different groupings depending on the activity. In a larger Year 2 class the teacher kept fairly stable groups. This was done to help the children to develop their collaborative skills, and to support the running of an integrated day. This teacher did provide opportunities for children from different groups to work together sometimes.

What are the likely effects of different grouping strategies, and can I deal with them?

The discussion on grouping in Chapter 4 led to the conclusion that mixed-ability grouping is most likely to lead to progress for all children. Yet many teachers use some form of grouping by ability some of the time. Grouping children according to their initial ideas is a form of ability grouping. Yet the same groups may not emerge each time the children are grouped, so there is likely to be some cross-fertilization of ideas. It was also clear from discussions with teachers that sometimes children were placed in particular groups for social, not academic, reasons. I suspect that the reason the research results in this area are so inconclusive is that different forms of grouping suit different situations.

In Chapter 4 I discussed grouping and the way girls and boys work in groups. In one of the case studies discussed in Chapter 5 the teacher consciously decided to group pupils in single-sex groups. She was aware that boys tend to monopolize equipment when carrying out experiments, particularly when the activities involve electrical equipment. In that case the class involved had little experience of collaborative work. The teacher needed to take on one or two issues at a time. Her main aim was confidence building and getting the children to think about what they were doing. In another class the teacher said that she had tried single-sex grouping, but had found it not to be appropriate. Instead she made the issue of gender explicit to the children. The phenomenon of 'bossy boys' was identified. The children were encouraged to deal with this as a group. In Chapter 4 I mentioned a multicultural Year 2 class, where a number of children with the same home language were taught. The teacher in that class was able to ensure that at least two children with a shared home language were placed in each group. This meant that the children could support one another by working together to explore the ideas in the lesson in both their home language and the language of instruction. This teacher's approach is supported by research that I discussed in Chapter 4. I identified research that suggested that children who are encouraged to explore ideas in the school and home languages tend to develop their liguistic competence just as well in the school language as they would have if restricted to speaking in the school language alone. They also develop their abilities in their home language. The provision of opportunities for mutual support by children in the class is not always possible, but where it is possible it can prove to be a valuable strategy.

Will the groups be fixed or will they change?

One of the case studies described in Chapter 5 showed how grouping, even within one topic, can shift and change according to the ideas children have and the rate at which their understanding develops. In the materials topic, the teacher of the class of 10 and 11 year olds started with three groups, two of similar ability range and one less able. By the end of the topic she had children working in ten different groups, most of whom were doing different things. This could only be achieved by planning lesson by lesson, based on assessments made during the lessons. It also required the teacher to listen carefully to the children during lessons, and to have a clear idea of what she wanted them to learn. In this way she was able to make decisions about where to direct individuals and groups. This required the teacher to know the children in the class extremely well. It also meant that she needed to be clear about what she could manage in terms of classroom organization. Teachers generally identify three or four groups of children, in terms of their ideas or in terms of social cohesion. This is not because children automatically fall neatly into such groups, or because the individuals in the group are all the same. It is probably because this is approximately the number a teacher can successfully cope with. This is an important consideration in deciding on the groups in the class.

Thus, when deciding on the way in which children will be grouped the teacher needs to consider how well different children work together. He or she must consider how the needs of particular individuals can best be served in the groups, what activities are planned and how much the teacher can cope with.

Classroom organization

How can I structure the sessions so that I can maximize the children's learning?

One of the daunting aspects of teaching science is the problem of organization. If the teacher was merely the facilitator in the classroom, then it would be fine to spend the lesson running round with a mop and providing additional resources. But teachers need to find time while children are doing science to teach them, to discuss ideas and to encourage them to engage in thinking deeply about what they are doing. One way to achieve this is to teach children to be independent learners. In most primary classrooms the children have access to equipment and books, leaving the teacher freer to work with individuals or groups.

Many teachers have routines established and strategies in place that enable the children to settle into work quickly. An example would be the use of planning boards and other structured worksheets which ensure that the children are used to a particular way of thinking through their work. These are essential to the smooth running of the classroom.

Sometimes, when I was observing a particular group working, I found it almost uncanny how the teacher seemed to know just when to return to a group to give support. Yet when I discussed it with the teacher it was clear that there was no magic involved: it had all been carefully thought out beforehand. Often this level of organization does not appear on the teacher's lesson plans, but it is clearly important to the running of the lesson. The teachers who were the most successful in providing differentiated learning opportunities were those who could describe, before the lesson, just how long particular activities would take and at what point in time they would need to be with a particular group. This takes a good deal of experience. A teacher at the beginning of a year, with an unfamiliar class of children, tends to be much more cautious about introducing a variety of activities. This is because predicting the times for such activities is more difficult until the teacher really gets to know the children.

Before starting on a particular topic a teacher needs to decide just how she or he will organize the classroom. These decisions need to be based on how well the teacher knows the class. The teacher needs to consider what the class is used to and how well the children in the class are able to work in a collaborative and independent manner. He or she must think about what the demands of the planned activities are on the teacher.

Providing access

How will I support those with reading and writing difficulties?

Many children who would otherwise find science fun and would learn a great deal through it are limited because of their reading and writing skills. A teacher who is clear about what it is she or he wants the children to learn from their science work is in a good position to find ways around the difficulties posed by reading and writing. A child can report findings orally to the teacher, or might take up options offered to make an annotated drawing. It is not always necessary to write up an experiment formally. One teacher used a shared planning board for a group of children to work on. This reduced the time any one individual had to put into writing. Furthermore, the use of standard recording devices, or standard phrases like 'this is how we will make it fair', means that children do not find the reading as demanding.

What range of tasks shall I set?

If all children in the class are asked to undertake the same task, then, unless the task is very open-ended, some children will find the work too demanding and some will not be stretched. Teachers might set all groups the same task but will then intervene to stretch the thinking of some and to support others. Children's initial ideas will provide clues about where they might go. As the topic progresses the teacher will need to take note of the children's ideas as they develop and be ready to offer interesting avenues for them to explore.

Are all the children likely to remain interested?

As a topic progresses, different questions are raised and some children may lose interest in the work. The teacher needs to be prepared with alternative activities that will promote progression in the concept area, but will interest that group of children. It may be that an individual needs to move away from investigations and into an exploration of the topic through secondary sources. Are the books available?

How can I get them to record?

Some topics seem to run and run. This is more often the case with younger children. In Key Stage 2, particularly in Years 5 and 6, there is so much to cover that a topic can fizzle out. In the case studies I present in this book I have not been able to describe ways in which topics reach a satisfactory conclusion. The whole issue of encouraging children to record their findings has not been looked at in any detail. Encouraging children to record can be a problem. Again, it comes back to providing children with a purpose, a reason for recording their findings. One way that many teachers use is to organize school assemblies or even special assemblies to which parents are invited. There is no reason why older children cannot enjoy this kind of activity.

Who are they communicating with?

A main reason for recording information is to communicate it to someone. Often recording is done by children because the teacher wants to see it. This can be demotivating for many children. Where children are engaged in different activities or investigations around the same topic there are opportunities for them to teach others in the class about their findings. This is motivating and valuable, as the learning opportunities are maximized. Other outcomes can be as articles for magazines or posters for a poster campaign. Then, on occasion, it might not be relevant to write up investigations, and children might use their new found knowledge to inform the design stage in some technology work. One example given in Chapter 4 was of a group of children writing a cartoon story in which they used their knowledge of building sites. The fact that they were working towards a useful product was highly motivating.

Ongoing assessment

Which strategies will suit the children and the topic?

Almost all the teachers I have mentioned in this book had strategies in place for gathering assessment information. Some, like the teacher working on the materials topic described in Chapter 5, identified specific times when they would be assessing their pupils. They generally informed the children that they were using a particular activity for assessment. The children were used to this. In other classes the teachers simply kept notes as they went along. In all cases it was important that opportunities for assessment were built into the teachers' plans. The teaching and the work of different groups were planned to take this into account. In several classes the teacher organized the groups so that only one or two groups were doing science at any one time. They were then able to identify, in the group activity, the points where

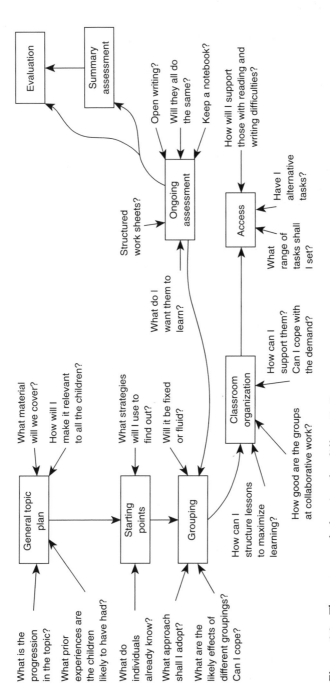

Figure 6.1 The process of planning for differentiation

they would be needed, either to provide some input or to assess the progress of individuals or groups. Where teachers were supported by classroom helpers, they organized the work to maximize the use of helpers and to release them to work in a more concerted way with other groups.

Final remarks

Differentiated learning experiences are not something that can be tagged on to a topic plan. It must inform all our teaching. It is part of the process of teaching. It remains a messy business. I have attempted to sum up the discussion above by plotting the process of developing differentiated teaching in Figure 6.1.

The teacher is the most important resource the children in a class have. Their learning is supported, interpreted, enhanced and applauded by the teacher. It is important that a teacher is always open to new ideas and is keen to explore new approaches to teaching. It is also important that a balance is kept between meeting the needs of the children and surviving to teach another day. This can be achieved by moving cautiously towards a goal, not rushing ahead changing everything. In England and Wales in recent years teachers have been forced to do too much rushing ahead. Over the next few years, I hope, there will be time for teachers to consolidate. In that time we need to think carefully about what we value in education. Addressing the needs of individuals should be a value we hold dear. Providing a rigorous well constructed science education has become a highly valued goal. Putting these two together will be an important step forward.

Bibliography

Alexander, R.J. (1984) *Primary Teaching*. Cassell: London.

Barnes, D. (1976) *From Communication to Curriculum*. Harmondsworth: Penguin.

Barnfield, M., Comber, M., Dyble, L., Farmer, M., Hagues, S., Hughes, S., Martin, T., McFarlane, C. and Moore, A. (1991) *Why on Earth? An Approach to Science with a Global Dimension at Key Stage 2*. Birmingham: Birmingham Development Education Centre.

Bassey, M. (1978) *Nine Hundred Primary School Teachers*. Slough: NFER.

Bath Science 5–16 (1992) *Exploring Science: Teachers' Resource Packs*. London: Thomas Nelson Ltd.

Bennet, N. (1987) Cooperative learning: children do it in groups; or do they? *Educational and Child Psychology*, 4(3): 7–18.

Bennet, N. and Cass, A. (1989) The effects of group composition on group interactive processes and pupil understanding. *British Educational Research Journal*, 15(1): 19–332.

Bentley, D. and Watts, M. (1994) *Primary Science and Technology*. Buckingham: Open University Press.

Black, P. and Harlen, W. (1993) How can we specify concepts for primary science, in P.J. Black and A.M. Lucas (eds) *Children's Informal Ideas in Science*. London: Routledge.

Black, P.J., Harlen, W., Russell, T., Bell, D., Hughes, A., Longden, K., Meadows, J., McGuigan, L., Osborne, J., Wadsworth, P. and Watt, D. (1993) *Nuffield Primary Science KS1 and 2 Curriculum Materials*. Edinburgh: Collins Educational.

Blyth, W.A.L. (1984) *Development, Experience and Curriculum in Primary Education*. London: Croom Helm.

Bolton Metropolitan Authority with CRIPSAT (1992) Children's understanding of science concepts. Unpublished research report by Teacher Group, Bolton Metropolitan Authority.

Browne, N. and France, P. (1985) 'Only cissies wear dresses': a look at sexist talk in the nursery, in G. Weiner (ed.) *Just a Bunch of Girls*, pp. 146–59. Milton Keynes: Open University Press.

Bruner, J.S. (1966) *Towards a Theory of Instruction*. Cambridge, MA: Harvard University Press.

Burgess, T. (1973) *Home and School*. London: Allen Lane.

Bush, A. (1956) Nature study in urban infant schools. *School Nature Study*, 203.

Caramazza, A., McCloskey, M. and Green, B. (1981) Naive beliefs in sophisticated subjects: misconceptions about trajectories of objects. *Cognition*, 9(2): 117–23.

Caravita, S. and Hallden, O. (1994) Re-framing the problem of conceptual change. *Learning and Instruction*, 4(1): 89–111.

Carey, S. (1987) *Conceptual Change in Childhood*. Boston and London: MIT Press.

Carré, C. and Ovens, C. (1994) *Science 7–11: Developing Primary Teaching Skills*. London: Routledge.

Carrington, B. and Short, G. (1989) *Race in the Primary School*. Windsor: NFER Nelson.

CATS (1991) *The Pilot Study of Standard Assessment Tasks for Key Stage 1: a Report by the Consortium for Assessment and Testing in Schools (CATS)*. London: SEAC.

Clayden, E. and Peacock, A. (1994) *Science for Curriculum Leaders*. London: Routledge.

CLIS (1984–91) *Children's Learning in Science Project Reports*. Leeds: Centre for the Study of Science and Mathematics Education.

Collins Primary Science (1990) *Teacher's Guide for Key Stage 1*. London: Collins Educational.

Contento, W. (1981) Children's thinking about food and eating: a Piagetian based study. *Journal of Nutrition and Eating Education*, 13: 86–90.

Crossley, J. (1991) Grouping for science. *Primary Science Review*, 17: 8–9.

Cummins, J. and Swain, M. (1986) *Bilingualism in Education*. London: Longman.

De Bóo, M. and Farnell, P. (1991) Equality – yes, but of what? *Primary Science Review*, 17: 18–19.

Dearing, Sir Ron (1993a) *The National Curriculum and Its Assessment: Interim Report.* York: National Curriculum Council.

Dearing, R. (1993b) *The National Curriculum and Its Assessment: Final Report.* London: SCAA.

Department of Education and Science (1978) *Primary Education in England: a Survey by HM Inspectors of Schools.* London: HMSO.

Department of Education and Science (1985) *Science 5–16: a Statement of Policy.* London: HMSO.

Department of Education and Science (1989a) *Science in the National Curriculum.* London: HMSO.

Department of Education and Science (1989b) *National Curriculum from Policy to Practice.* London: HMSO.

Department for Education (1995) *Science in the National Curriculum.* London: HMSO.

Donaldson, M. (1978) *Children's Minds.* London: Fontana.

Duggan, S. and Gott, R. (1994) The place of investigations in practical work in the UK National Curriculum for science. *International Journal for Science Education,* 16(3): 121–30.

Evans, N. (1994) Educare the only policy. *Primary Science Review,* 35: 21–2.

Feasey, R. (1994) The challenge of science, in C. Aubrey (ed.) *The Role of Subject Knowledge in Early Years Schooling.* London: Falmer Press.

Forde, F., Hall, L. and McClean, V. (1988) *The Real McCoy: Black Makers of History.* London: The Book Place, ALBSU edition.

Galton, M. (1995) *Crisis in the Primary Classroom.* London: David Fulton.

George, J. and Glasgow, J. (1988) Street science and conventional science in the West Indies. *Studies in Science Education,* 15: 109–18.

Gesell, A. and Ilg, F. I. (1965) *The Child from Five to Ten.* London: Hamish Hamilton.

Gott, R. and Mashiter, J. (1994) Practical work in science: a task-based approach, in R. Levinson (ed.) *Teaching Science.* London: Routledge.

Grant, M. and Givens, N. (1984) A sense of purpose: approaching CDT through social issues. *Studies in Design Education, Craft and Technology,* 16(2): 94–8.

Grant, M. and Harding, J. (1987) Changing the polarity. *International Journal of Science Education,* 9(3): 335–42.

Gunstone, R.F., Gray, C.M. and Searle, P. (1992) Some long term effects of uninformed conceptual change. *Science Education,* 76(2): 175–97.

Hadow Report (1931) *Report of the Consultative Committee on the Primary School.* London: HMSO.

Hanson, D. and Qualter, A. (1995) Nepali children's understanding of 'alive'. *Primary Science Review,* 38: 26–8.

Harlen, W. (1975) *Science 5–13: a Formative Evaluation.* London: Macmillan Education.

Harlen, W. (1978) Does content matter in primary science? *School Science Review*, 59: 614–25.

Harlen, W. (1985) Helping children to plan investigations, in W. Harlen (ed.) *Primary Science: Taking the Plunge.* pp. 58–74. London: Heinemann.

Harlen, W. (1993) *Teaching and Learning in Primary Science.* London: Paul Chapman Publishers.

Harlen, W., Macro, C., Schilling, M., Malvern, D. and Reed, K. (1990) *Progress in Primary Science.* London: Routledge.

Hendly, D., Parkinson, J., Stables, A. and Tanner, H. (1995) Attitudes to the National Curriculum Foundation subjects of English, mathematics, science and technology in Key Stage 3 in South Wales. *Educational Studies*, 21(1): 85–97.

Horbury, A. and Pears, H. (1994) Collaborative groupwork: how infant children can manage it. *Education 3–13*, 22(3): 20–8.

Jannikos, M. (1995) Are the stereotyped views of scientists being brought into the 90s? *Primary Science Review*, 37: 26–8.

Jelly, S.J. (1985) Helping children to raise questions – and answering them, in W. Harlen (ed.) *Primary Science: Taking the plunge*, pp. 47–57. London: Heinemann.

Jorde, D. and Lea, A. (1987) The primary science project in Norway, in *Proceedings of Fourth GASAT Conference*, pp. 66–72. Ann Arbor: University of Michigan.

Kay, B.W. (1978) Monitoring pupils' performance, in D. Hopkinson (ed.) *Standards and the School Curriculum: Analysis and Suggestions from HM Inspectorate*, pp. 25–33. London: Ward-Lock.

Kelly, A. (1987) Does the train set matter? Scientific hobbies and science achievement and choice, in *Contributions to the Fourth GASAT Conference.* Ann Arbor: University of Michigan.

Kimbell, R., Stables, K., Wheeler, T., Wosniak, T. and Kelly, V. (1991) *The Assessment of Performance in Design and Technology.* London: School Examination and Assessment Council.

Kirby, N. (1981) *Personal Values in Primary Education.* London: Harper & Row.

Lewis A. (1992) From planning to practice. *British Journal of Special Education*, 19: 24–7.

Lucas, A.M. Linke, R.D. and Sedgewick, P.P. (1979) School children's criteria for 'alive': a content analysis approach. *Journal of Psychology*, 103: 103–12.

Lynch, P.P. and Jones, B.L. (1995) Students' alternative frameworks: towards a linguistic and cultural interpretation. *International Journal of Science Education*, 17(1): 107–18.

McGarvey, B., Day, J. and Harper, D. (1993) *Differentiated Learning in Science: Project Report.* Coleraine: NICC, Faculty of Education, University of Coleraine.

McGuigan, L. (1990) Words, words, words. *Primary Science Review*, 14: 32–3.

McGuigan, L., Russell, T. and Qualter, A. (1994) Coverage: competing considerations in implementing science in the National Curriculum KS1–3. Paper presented at BERA Conference, Oxford, September.

McNamara, D. (1991) Subject knowledge and its application: problems and possibilities for teacher educators. *Journal of Education for Teaching*, 17(2): 113–28.

Mali, G.B. and Howe, A. (1979) Development of earth and gravity concepts among Nepali children. *Science Education*, 63(5): 685–91.

Massey, I. (1991) *More than Skin Deep*. London: Hodder and Stoughton.

Møller Andersen, A. and Sørensen, H. (1995) Action research and teacher development in Denmark – towards a gender inclusive classroom. Paper presented at the European Conference of Science Education, Leeds University, April.

Mortimore, P., Simmons, P., Stoll, L., Lewis, D. and Ecob, R. (1988) *School Matters: the Junior Years*. Hove: Lawrence Earlbaum Associates.

Murphy, P. (1989) Gender and assessment in science, in P. Murphy and B. Moon (eds) *Developments in Learning and Assessment*, pp. 323–6. London: Hodder and Stoughton.

Murphy, P. (1994) Gender differences in pupils' reactions to practical work, in R. Levinson (ed.) *Teaching Science*, pp. 131–42. Routledge: London.

National Curriculum Council (1989) *Science Non-Statutory Guidance*. York: NCC.

National Curriculum Council (1991) *NCC INSET Resources. Science Explorations*. York: NCC.

National Foundation for Educational Research/Bishop Grossteste College (NFER/BGC) (1991) *The Pilot Study for Standard Assessment Tasks for Key Stage 1: a Report by NFER/BGC Consortium*. London: SEAC.

Newton, L.D. and Newton, D. (1991) Child's view of a scientist. *Questions Magazine*, 4(1): 20–1.

Nias, J. (1989) *Primary Teachers Talking*. Routledge: London.

Nuffield Foundation (1967) *Nuffield Junior Science: Teacher's Guide 1 and 2*. London: William Collins.

Nuffield Primary Science (1993) *Key Stage 1 and Key Stage 2 Teacher's Guides*. London: Collins Educational.

Nussbaum, J. (1985) The Earth as a cosmic body, in R. Driver, E. Guesne and A. Tiberghien (eds) *Children's Ideas in Science*. Milton Keynes: Open University Press.

OFSTED (1994) *Science and Mathematics in Schools: a Review*. London: HMSO.

OFSTED (1995) *Science: a Review of Inspection Findings 1993/94. A Report from the Office of Her Majesty's Chief Inspector of Schools*. London: HMSO.

O'Loughlin, M. (1992) Rethinking science education: beyond Piagetian constructivism, towards a sociocultural model of teaching and learning. *Journal of Research into Science Teaching*, 29(8): 791–829.

Osborne, J.F., Black, P., Meadows, J. and Smith, M. (1993) Young children's ideas about light and their development. *International Journal of Science Education*, 15(1): 83–93.

Osborne, J., Wadsworth, P. and Black, P. (1992) *Processes of Life. Primary SPACE Research Reports.* Liverpool: Liverpool University Press.

Osborne, R. and Freyberg, P. (1985) *Learning in Science: the Implications of Children's Science.* London: Heinemann.

Oxford Primary Science (1993) *Teacher's Guide Key Stage 1.* Oxford: Oxford University Press.

Parker, L.H. and Offer, J.A. (1987) School science achievement: conditions for equality. *International Journal of Science Education*, 9(3): 263–9.

Peacock, A. (ed.) (1991) *Science in Primary Schools: the Multicultural Dimension.* Routledge: London.

Piaget, J. (1929) *The Child's Conception of the World.* London: Routledge and Kegan Paul.

Plowden Report (1967) *Children and Their Primary Schools*, Report of the Central Advisory Council for Education (England), Vol 1. London: HMSO.

Posner, G.J., Strike, K.A., Hewson, P.W. and Gerzog, W.A. (1982) Accommodation of scientific concepts: towards a theory of conceptual change. *Science Education*, 66: 211–17.

Qualter, A. (1992) I would like to know more about that: a study of the interest shown by girls and boys in scientific topics. *International Journal of Science Education*, 15(3): 307–17.

Qualter, A. (1994a) Where does electricity come from? *Primary Science Review*, 35: 20–2.

Qualter, A. (1994b) MANWEB Primary Technology: an evaluation of an industry funded project. Unpublished report for MANWEB.

Qualter, A. (1996) Teacher training in primary science – the challenge for the future. *British Journal of In Service Education*, in the press.

Qualter, A., Francis, C., Boyes, E. and Stanisstreet, M. (1995) The greenhouse effect: what do primary children think? *Education 3–13*, 23(2): 28–31.

Qualter, A., Strang, J., Swatton, P. and Taylor, R. (1990) *Exploration. A Way of Learning Science.* Oxford: Blackwell.

Randall, G. (1985) Classroom interactions in workshops and laboratories. Contributions to the Third GASAT Conference, Chelsea College, University of London.

Rennie, L.J. and Parker, L.H. (1987) Detecting and accounting for gender differences in mixed-sex and single-sex groupings in science lessons. *Educational Review*, 39(1): 65–73.

Richardson, R. (1995) Spot the difference. *Child Education*, April: 21–3.

Rush, L. (1995) An evaluation of the implementation of a school development plan in one primary school. Unpublished MEd Dissertation, Liverpool University.

Russell, T., Bell, D., Longden, K. and McGuigan, L. (1993) *Rocks, Soil and Weather. Primary SPACE Research Reports*. Liverpool: Liverpool University Press.

Russell, T., Black, P., Harlen, W., Johnson, S. and Palacio, D. (1988) *Science at Age 11: a Review of APU Survey Findings 1980–84*. London: HMSO.

Russell, T., Qualter, A. and McGuigan, L. (1994) *Evaluation of the Implementation of Science in the National Curriculum Key Stages 1, 2 and 3*, Vols 1, 2 and 3. London: Schools Curriculum and Assessment Authority.

Russell, T. and Watt, D. (1990) *Growth: Primary SPACE Project Research Reports*. Liverpool: Liverpool University Press.

SCAA (School Curriculum and Assessment Authority) (1995) *Planning the Curriculum at Key Stages 1 and 2*. London: SCAA.

Schilling, M., Atkinson, H., Boyes, E., Qualter, A. and Russell, T. (1991) *Understanding Science: Forces*. York: NCC.

Scholfield, B., Bell, J., Black, P., Johnson, S., Murphy, P., Qualter, A. and Russell, T. (1989) *Science at Age 13: a Review of APU Survey Findings 1980–84*. London: HMSO.

Science Teacher's Joint Sub-Committee (1959) *Science in the Primary School*. London: John Murray.

Science 5–13 (1972–5) *Units for Teacher. Working with Wood*. London: Macdonald.

Selly, N. (1994) Cats in the dark. *Primary Science Review*, 34: 17–18.

Shorrocks, D., Frobisher, L., Nelson, N., Turner, L. and Waterson, A. (1993) *Implementing National Curriculum Assessment in the Primary School*. London: Hodder and Stoughton.

Shullman, L. (1986) Those who understand: knowledge growth in teaching. *Educational Research*, 15: 4–14.

Simon, B. (1981) Why no pedagogy in England?, in B. Simon and W. Taylor (eds) *Education in the Eighties, the Central Issues*, pp. 124–45. London: Batsford.

Slavin, R. (1983) *Cooperative Learning*. London: Methuen.

Smith, R. (1994) Richer or poorer, better or worse? How has the development of primary science teaching been affected by National Curriculum policy? *Curriculum Journal*, 5(2): 163–77.

Sneider, C. and Pulos, S. (1983) Children's cosmographies, understanding the Earth's shape and gravity. *Science Education*, 67(2): 205–21.

Sorsby, B., Bury, K. and Gibbons, H. (1992) Why did she sink? A cross curricular study of the Mary Rose. *Primary Science Review*, 21: 24–5.

STAIR (1991) *The Pilot Study of Standard Assessment Tasks for Key Stage 1: a Report by the STAIR Consortium.* London: SEAC.

Thorp, S. (ed.) (1991) *Race, Equality and Science Teaching: an Active INSET Manual for Teachers and Educators.* Hatfield: ASE.

Trowbridge, J.E. and Mintses, J.J. (1985) Students' alternative conceptions of animals and animal classification. *School Science and Maths,* 85: 304–16.

Troyna, B. and Farrow, S. (1991) Science for all? Antiracism, science and the primary school, in A. Peacock (ed.) *Science in Primary Schools: the Multicultural Dimension.* Routledge: London.

Versey, J., Fairbrother, R.W., Parkin, T., Bourne, J., Dye, A. and Watkinson, A. (undated) *Differentiation: Managing Differentiated Learning and Assessment in the National Curriculum (Science).* Hatfield: ASE.

Wadsworth, P., referred to in Murphy, P. and Scanlon, E. (1994) *E880: Teaching in Primary Schools. Primary Module 1 – Science.* Milton Keynes: Open University.

Watt, D. and Russell, T.R. (1990) *Sound: Primary SPACE Research Reports.* Liverpool: Liverpool University Press.

Watts, D. (1983) A study of school children's alternative frameworks of the concept of force. *European Journal of Science Education,* 5(2): 217–30.

Webb, G. and Qualter, A. (1996) Differentiation in primary science: a case study in complexity. *Education 3–13,* in the press.

Weston, P. (1992) A decade of differentiation. *British Journal of Special Education,* 19(1): 6–9.

Willson, S. and Willson, M. (1994) Concept mapping as an assessment tool. *Primary Science Review,* 34: 14–16.

Wittrock, M.C. (1974) Learning as a generative process. *Educational Psychology,* 11: 87–95.

Wood, D. (1988) *How Children Think and Learn.* Oxford: Blackwell.

Wright, C. (1987) *Black Students – White teachers,* in B. Troyna (ed.) *Inequality in Education.* London: Tavistock.

Index

PRIMARY SCIENCE AND TECHNOLOGY
PRACTICAL ALTERNATIVES

Di Bentley and Mike Watts (eds)

This book explores the ways in which science and technology can take place in the early and middle years at school. At the heart of the book are a number of case studies of actual practice drawn from primary schools in action. These studies contribute to a theoretical approach grounded in children's learning, and are used in exploring the real problems of planning, management, organization, teaching and learning as classroom practitioners try to implement new curriculum directives. The chapters examine the nature of learning experiences, the practice of teaching, teaching for specific skills, the role of the specialist coordinator, assessment and record keeping, scientific and technological problem solving and working for equal opportunities. The authors draw on their own wide experience in science education and upon their work with teachers in primary classrooms.

Contents

Building on experience – Learning and conceptual change – Conceptual development and language – School planning for conceptual change – Planning for the curriculum and the classroom – Classroom organization and management – Posing problems: effective questioning – Solving problems in science and technology – Working for equal opportunities – Teacher assessment – Being a co-ordinator – Teacher knowledge and teacher education – Appendices – References – Index.

Contributors

Steve Alsop, Brenda Barber, Di Bentley, Rosemary Denman, Catherine Ducheck, Jane Eaton, B. Hodgson, Jenny McGivern, Sue Marran, P. Murphy, Cindy Palmer, Pauline Prince, Jenny Saady, E. Scanlon, Amanda Walsh, Mike Watts, Virginia Whitby, Elizabeth Whitelegg, Doreen Wootton.

240pp   0 335 19028 6 (paperback)   0 335 19029 4 (hardback)

ORGANIZING FOR LEARNING IN THE PRIMARY CLASSROOM
A BALANCED APPROACH TO CLASSROOM MANAGEMENT

Janet R. Moyles

What is it that underlies classroom organization, routines, rules, structures and daily occurrences? What are the prime objectives and what influences the decisions of teachers and children? What is it useful for teachers to consider when contemplating the issues of classroom management and organization? What do different practices have to offer?

Organizing for Learning in the Primary Classroom explores the whole range of influences and values which underpin *why* teachers do *what* they do in the classroom context and what these mean to children and others. Janet Moyles examines teaching and learning styles, children's independence and autonomy, coping with children's differences, the physical classroom context and resources, time management and ways of involving others in the day-to-day organization. Practical suggestions are given for considering both the functional and aesthetic aspects of the classroom context. Opportunities are provided for teachers to reflect on their own organization and also consider innovative and flexible ways forward to deal with new and ever increasing demands on their time and sanity!

> This book is to be highly recommended for all primary school teachers . . .
>
> *(Management in Education)*

> . . . indispensable to courses in initial teacher education and to providers of inset.
>
> *(Child Education)*

> Janet Moyles brings her long experience of the primary school to *Organizing for Learning in the Primary Classroom* . . . I particularly like the attention she gives to the physical environment, giving lots of advice about arrangements of furniture and the role of the teacher's desk . . .
>
> *(Times Educational Supplement)*

Contents

208pp   0 335 15659 2 (Paperback)   0 335 15660 6 (Hardback)